Linda's Kitchen

Linda's Kitchen

SIMPLE AND INSPIRING RECIPES FOR MEALS WITHOUT MEAT

LINDA McCARTNEY

Food Consultant
Rosamond Richardson

Photography
Debbie Patterson

A Bulfinch Press Book
Little, Brown and Company
Boston   New York   Toronto   London

*To my family and all veggies,
present and future*

Like all diets, a vegetarian diet should be a balanced one.
If you have any doubts or concern about whether your diet is suitable
you should consult your doctor. Additionally, if you have allergies
you should not use those recipes that contain ingredients to which you
may be allergic or otherwise affected.

Introduction copyright © 1995 by MPL Communications Ltd
Text and Photographs copyright © 1995 by
Little, Brown and Company (Inc.)

First Edition
Reprinted 1995

ISBN 0-316-87735-2 (hardback)
ISBN 0-316-87881-2 (paperback)

Library of Congress Catalog Card Number 95–75416
A CIP catalogue for this book is available
from the British Library

Food styling: Jane Suthering
Designer: Janet James

Published simultaneously in the United States of America
by Bulfinch Press, an imprint and trademark of
Little, Brown and Company (Inc.),
in Great Britain by Little, Brown and Company (UK)
and in Canada by Little, Brown & Company (Canada) Limited

The author would like to thank Paul, Heather, Mary, Stella,
James, Louise, Robby and team, Viv and team, Carol Judy and team,
Geoff, Pat, Sherrie, Marie, Sue, Shelagh, Louise, Laura,
Monique, Ann, Mike, Ian, Tim and team, John, Sharon, Maxine, and
everyone who helped and shared a veggie recipe.

The publishers would like to thank Laura Ashley for permission
to reproduce the fabric used on the cover (Glenisla Check
in cowslip; for further information call 01628 770345) and Ian Mankin
for permission to reproduce that used in the menu planners
(Carlton Plaid in mustard; for further information call 0171 371 8825).

The photograph on page one features edible flower garnishes
(see page 147)

PRINTED AND BOUND IN GERMANY

CONTENTS

INTRODUCTION....................................6

MENU PLANNERS, BY SEASON..................8

THE RECIPES

Soups...16

Light Meals and Side Dishes 32

Main Courses.....................................54

Pasta, Rice and Potatoes 84

Pastry 108

Barbecues...118

Salads 128

Sauces and Dips 148

Desserts, Cakes and Biscuits 158

Pastry Basics 178

VEGETARIAN QUESTIONS & ANSWERS.......180

THE VEGETARIAN PANTRY....................184

NUTRITION FOR VEGETARIANS 187

INDEX..190

V INDICATES A VEGAN DISH

$\mathcal{I}$ntroduction

When my husband asked me why I was writing another cookbook, it made me realize how time had flown – and how far vegetarian cuisine had progressed in the intervening years. When I wrote my first cookbook, it was to show my family and friends how easy it was to become a vegetarian. But now our eating habits have changed, most of us are trying to cut down on fatty foods, and I felt the time had come to bring things up to date and to increase the range of easily prepared recipes that are available to today's cook.

Even if you find cooking daunting, I hope to bring out the creative cook in you. It may be that you've always thought of vegetarian meals as tiresome to prepare and bland in taste – in which case there's a surprise in store for you. Vegetarian cooking is easy, it's tasty, and it's good for your body too. Recent research has shown that a vegetarian diet can dramatically lessen the risk of – amongst other things – heart disease, angina, cancer, diabetes and high blood pressure.

Some people believe that they are vegetarian if they just cut out red meat, but a vegetarian eats no meat, and no fish either. If you go veggie, it means no animal dies for your plate. I've met a lot of people who say, "I'm almost veggie, but I still eat fish." To me that's like being "almost pregnant" – either you are or you aren't. I know that for some people cutting out fish is the most difficult obstacle on the road to vegetarianism. But fish have feelings too, and anyone who has ever seen a fish hooked out of the water, jerking and gasping for breath, should realize that. The "bountiful sea" does *not* exist for us to plunder at will, and perhaps if we started thinking in terms of sea*life* instead of sea*food* our appetite for fish might be lost.

Of course tradition is responsible for much of today's meaty diet. For most of us in the West, meat and two veg is a standard meal and, for many people, Sundays are not complete without a roast meat dinner. But the world has changed since those traditions developed. Many more people share this planet and, as the population grows, it is simply not going to be possible to feed everyone on a meat-based diet. There just isn't enough grazing land for all the livestock required.

For me, that's a good enough reason in itself for becoming a vegetarian – because if we fed the starving people of the world the grain we use to fatten farm animals there really could be enough to go round. If everyone in the West reduced their meat consumption by just ten per cent, it would free up enough grazing land to grow food for up to 40 million people. So, being a vegetarian is not only better for you, it's better for everyone.

There are other lives that will be saved if you go veggie – the lives of the millions of animals that are slaughtered every year. Butchered in such horrific ways that if slaughterhouses had glass walls, we'd all be vegetarian. So, be a life-saver and a world-saver, and start a whole new way of life.

There are meals for all to enjoy here – from vegan meals to meals for the truck driver who reckons he'd miss his meat (…but he won't), to kids' meals, low-calorie meals, meals for entertaining and family meals including a vegetarian Sunday lunch. While you're cooking, don't be afraid to adapt these recipes to suit yourself. I've tried to make taste the main ingredient in all of them; so get into the kitchen, rattle those pots and pans, have fun, and save lives while you're doing it – yours, the animals' and the planet's.

Linda McCartney

MENU PLANNER

A Dinner Party for 8

CHEESE PALMIERS 48

AVOCADO, MOZZARELLA AND TOMATO SALAD (x2) 134

SPAGHETTINI WITH SUN-DRIED TOMATOES, AUBERGINES AND CHILLI (x2) 90

SPECIAL ROCKET SALAD WITH SPINACH AND PARMESAN (x2) 129

LEMON SOUFFLÉ TART 167

A Family Lunch for 4 v

ASPARAGUS SOUP 25

CRISPY MUSHROOM LAYERS 71

WATERCRESS SALAD WITH GARLIC CROUTONS 136

FRUIT SORBET 160

A Supper for 4

COURGETTE AND WATERCRESS SOUP 26

AUBERGINE AND HERB CASSEROLE (halved) 66

GARLIC MASHED POTATOES 106

LEMON GREEN BEANS 44

An Easter Menu for 10

ASPARAGUS WITH GARLIC (x3) 44
OR WITH HOLLANDAISE (x2) 150

CREAMY VEGETABLE PIE (x2) 112

NOODLE BAKE (x2) 60

SAUTÉ OF SWEET POTATOES (x4) 105

SHREDDED COURGETTE SALAD (x2) 141

CHOCOLATE DELIGHT 163

MOUSSE MADE WITH LEMONS 160

FOR SPRING

A Light Buffet for 20

PARTY EGGS (x3) 49

CRISP FILO MUSHROOM PARCELS 50

FILO CHEESE STRAWS (x2) 48

CHEESE AND NUT PÂTÉ (x2) 47

STUFFED PEPPERS (x3) 68

CHEESE AND BROCCOLI TART (x2) 115

SPICY RAW MUSHROOM SALAD (x2) 136

CAESAR SALAD (x2) 133

TECHNICOLOR BEAN SALAD 142

....

PECAN PIE (x2) 166

CHEESECAKE MADE WITH BLACKCURRANTS 166

A French Menu for 4

WARM GOAT'S CHEESE SALAD 133

....

VEGETABLE MILLE-FEUILLES WITH PESTO 116

SCALLOPED POTATOES 107

PROVENÇAL PEPPER SALAD 139

....

CRÈME BRÛLÉE 163

A Chinese Menu for 6

VEGETABLE SPRING ROLLS 110

STIR-FRY OF SPRING VEGETABLES WITH NOODLES (x1½) 56

RICE NOODLES WITH BROCCOLI, GINGER AND GARLIC 93

CHINESE EGG FRIED RICE 94

SWEET AND SOUR SAUCE 153

....

MANGO SORBET 160

A Birthday Party for 4

CRISP FILO MUSHROOM PARCELS 50

....

GOAT'S CHEESE AND DILL SOUFFLÉ 82

....

PASTA TWISTS WITH SPINACH AND NUTS 88

CAESAR SALAD 133

....

CHOCOLATE VICTORIA SPONGE WITH CHOCOLATE BUTTER ICING 175 DECORATED WITH CANDLES AND FLOWERS

MENU PLANNER

A Teenagers' Party for 15

PARTY EGGS (x1½) 49

FILO CHEESE STRAWS (x2) 48

MEXICAN CORN BREAD (x2) 34

NACHOS (x2) 33

EASY PIZZA 117

TASTY BEANBURGERS (x4) 55

LIGHT SAUSAGE ROLLS (x2) 49

CRISPY POTATO SKINS (x2) 105

CARROT SALAD 134

AMERICAN SOURED CREAM DIP 156 WITH TORTILLA CHIPS

....

CHOCOLATE CHIP COOKIES 176

BAKED CHOCOLATE PUDDING WITH CHOCOLATE FUDGE SAUCE (x2) 162

CARROT CAKE 172

A Barbecue for 12

DILL CUCUMBER DIP (x2) 156 WITH CRUDITÉS

AMERICAN SOURED CREAM DIP 156

....

MARINATED VEGETARIAN SAUSAGES AND BURGERS (x2) 119

CRUSTY GARLIC POTATOES (x2) 125

VEGETABLE KEBABS (x2) 119

CHAR-GRILLED MUSHROOMS WITH ROSEMARY AND GARLIC (x2) 120

COURGETTES WITH HERBS (x2) 124

MEXICAN CORN BREAD (x2) 34

BARBECUE SAUCE 153

SALSAS 152

ROASTED RED PEPPER SAUCE 149

TARRAGON AND MUSTARD SAUCE 149

SELECTION OF SALADS

....

PEACHES AND BUTTERSCOTCH 127

PRALINE BANANAS (x2) 127

A Lunch for 6

SUMMERY TOMATO SOUP WITH DILL 28

....

TAGLIATELLE WITH MUSHROOM SAUCE (x1½) 88

CARROT SALAD 134

MIXED LEAF SALAD WITH LEMONY CAPER VINAIGRETTE 147

....

FROZEN VANILLA MOUSSE (x2) 159

OAT AND RAISIN BISCUITS 177

A Romantic Dinner for 2
(halve all recipes)

AUBERGINE CAVIAR 40

....

VEGETABLE SOUFFLÉ 82

ROSTI 107

SPECIAL ROCKET SALAD WITH SPINACH AND PARMESAN 129

....

TIRAMISÙ 162

FOR SUMMER

A Buffet for 24

GREEN HERB DIP 157
WITH CRUDITÉS

AUBERGINE CAVIAR (x2) 40

MUSHROOM
TRIANGLES (x6) 50

SUMMER LASAGNE (x2) 85

LAYERED VEGETABLE
TERRINE (x2) 81

LIGHT SPINACH AND CHEESE
PIE (x2) 113

LEMON
GREEN BEANS (x3) 44

SIMPLE
SAFFRON RICE (x2) 94

FENNEL SALAD 134

CURRIED
PASTA SALAD 144

GREEN BEAN SALAD 141

POTATO AND COS
LETTUCE WITH GARLIC
VINAIGRETTE 130

CHEESECAKE MADE WITH
STRAWBERRIES 166

CHOCOLATE MOUSSE (x2) 159

APPLE PIE 170

A Dinner Party for 8

GARDEN SOUP WITH
PESTO (x2) 26

MELTING AUBERGINES
(x2) 40

QUICK MEATLESS
STROGANOFF (x2) 68
WITH RICE

COURGETTES WITH
SWEETCORN (x2) 43

WATERCRESS
SALAD WITH GARLIC
CROUTONS (x2) 136

RASPBERRY MOUSSE 160

CRISPY GINGER NUTS 176

An Anniversary Celebration for 12

RUSSIAN BORSCHT (x2) 22

CAESAR SALAD (x2) 133

SAVOURY VEGETABLE
STRUDEL (x2) 110

SPINACH
FUSILLI BAKE (x2) 92

VEGETABLE PURÉE:
CARROT (x2) 46

POTATO AND COS LETTUCE
WITH GARLIC VINAIGRETTE
(x2) 130

BLUEBERRY TART (x2) 168

A Mediterranean Menu for 4

ARTICHOKE DIP 157

TUSCAN BEAN AND
CABBAGE SOUP 19

PENNE WITH TOMATOES
AND MOZZARELLA 89

PROVENÇAL PEPPER
SALAD 139

CHOCOLATE MOUSSE 159

MENU PLANNER

A Halloween Supper for 10

CRISPY POTATO SKINS
(x2) 105
WITH DIPS 156–7

PUMPKIN SOUP (x2) 20

BAKED SWEETCORN
PUDDING (x2) 60
MACARONI SPECIAL (x2) 93
CURRIED CHICK PEAS
WITH ONIONS (x2) 75
SPANISH RICE (x2) 97
SELECTION OF SALADS

APPLE PIE (x2) 170

A Brunch for 4

FRUIT JUICES 52

SPANISH OMELETTE 83
LIGHT SAUSAGE ROLLS 49
MEXICAN CORN BREAD 34
SERVED WITH GRILLED
TOMATOES, GRILLED
MUSHROOMS AND FRIED
BREAD

A Mexican Party for 8

GUACAMOLE 157
SALSAS 152
NACHOS 33

SPICY REFRIED BEAN
TACOS (x2) 35
QUESADILLAS (x8) 33
CHEESE ENCHILADAS
(x1½) 39
TACOS WITH TOMATOES
AND VEGETARIAN MINCE 34

ORANGE OR
LEMON SORBET 160

A Thanksgiving Dinner for 10

POTATO AND CARROT SOUP
(x1½) 17

MEATLESS LOAF 62
WITH YORKSHIRE
PUDDINGS 63
AND GRAVY 155
CREAMY POTATO AND
LEEK BAKE (x4) 102
COURGETTES WITH
SWEETCORN (x2) 43
SELECTION OF SALADS

PLUM COBBLER 168
CHOCOLATE DELIGHT 163

FOR AUTUMN

A Birthday Party
for 6

**LAYERED VEGETABLE
TERRINE 81**
WILD MUSHROOM SAUCE 154

**SPINACH FETTUCCINE
WITH TOMATOES AND
BASIL (x2) 89**
**LEMON
GREEN BEANS (x2) 44**
**SPECIAL ROCKET SALAD
WITH SPINACH AND
PARMESAN 129**

**CARROT CAKE 172
DECORATED WITH CANDLES
AND FLOWERS**

A Family Supper
for 4

**MUSHROOM
TRIANGLES 50**

**LANCASHIRE HOT POT
WITH BUTTER BEANS 61**
NOODLE BAKE 60
CAESAR SALAD 133

**APPLE SPONGE
PUDDING 170**

A Lunch for 4

SWEETCORN CHOWDER 25

CHILLI NON CARNE 55
PERSIAN CHILAU RICE 96
**POTATO AND COS
LETTUCE WITH GARLIC
VINAIGRETTE 130**

BLUEBERRY TART 168

A Greek Menu
for 6

**ASPARAGUS
WITH GARLIC (x1½) 44**

**MUSHROOM
MOUSSAKA 70**
**GREEK RICE
WITH LEEKS (x1½) 96**
FENNEL SALAD 134

**FROZEN MOUSSE
MADE WITH GREEK YOGURT
AND FRUIT (x2) 159**

MENU PLANNER

A Lunch for 4

LENTIL SOUP 17

....

**STUFFED
BAKED POTATOES 101**
**WATERCRESS SALAD WITH
GARLIC CROUTONS 136**

....

LEMON DRIZZLE CAKE 175

An Indian Menu
for 6

**MUSHROOM TRIANGLES
(x1½) 50**

**SIMPLE VEGETABLE
CURRY (x2) 74**

**EASY CAULIFLOWER
DHAL 74**

**POTATO AND AUBERGINE
CURRY (x2) 102**

**CURRIED CHICK PEAS
WITH ONIONS (x1½) 75**

**SIMPLE SAFFRON RICE
(x1½) 94**

....

MANGO SORBET 160

Two Family
Suppers for 3-4

**MEATLESS MEATBALLS 73
WITH SPAGHETTI
AND RICH TOMATO
SAUCE 151**
**GREEN SALAD WITH GARLIC
MUSTARD DRESSING 146**

....

BAKEWELL TART 167

....

CLASSIC PASTIES 112
RICH TOMATO SAUCE 151
**STUFFED
BAKED POTATOES 101**
STEAMED VEGETABLES

....

**COBBLER MADE WITH
APPLES 168**

A Christmas
Dinner for 10

VEGETABLE SOUP (x1½) 19

....

**COTTAGE CRUNCH
CASSEROLE (x1½) 67**
GRAVY 155
**CHEESE AND PARSLEY
SAUCE (x2) 155**
**SCALLOPED POTATOES
(x2) 107**
STEAMED VEGETABLES
**COURGETTES WITH
SWEETCORN (x3) 43**
**VEGETABLE PURÉE:
CARROT AND PARSNIP
(x1½) 46**

....

LEMON SOUFFLÉ TART 167
CRÈME BRÛLÉE 163

FOR WINTER

A New Year's Celebration for 10

EASY LEEK PUFFS (x3) 116

SPINACH PANCAKES WITH
MUSHROOMS (x2½) 79

RISOTTO (x2) 99
MADE WITH
VEGETABLES OF CHOICE

CAULIFLOWER SALAD
WITH MUSTARD
MAYONNAISE (x2) 140

BEETROOT SALAD 140

SPONGE PUDDING WITH
APRICOTS AND ALMONDS
(x3) 171

A Dinner Party for 6

PASTA AND BEAN SALAD
WITH BASIL
AND PECORINO 142

WINTER LASAGNE 92
GREEN SALAD WITH
BALSAMIC GARLIC AND
HERB DRESSING 146

FLOATING ISLANDS 171

Sunday Lunch for 6 non-veggies

CRISPY POTATO SKINS
(x1½) 105
WITH FAVOURITE DIPS

TOAD-IN-THE-HOLE 63
LEMON
GREEN BEANS (x2) 44
POTATO AND CABBAGE
MASH (x2) 106
GRAVY 155

APPLE SPONGE PUDDING 170

A Dinner Party for 4 ♥

GREEN SOUP
WITH PARSLEY 22

CRISPY MUSHROOM
LAYERS 71
GARLIC MASHED
POTATOES 106
CARROT SALAD 134
STEAMED GREEN
VEGETABLES

FRUIT SORBET 160

VEGAN FRUIT CAKE 172

CHAPTER ONE

Soups

O ne of the joys of cooking without meat is making soups through the seasons, using the abundant harvest of fresh ingredients with their varied colours, flavours and textures. The first baby vegetables appear in the spring, to enliven lighter soups; then come summer favourites like courgettes and sweetcorn. Autumn brings squashes, pumpkins and artichokes, which make superlative soups; and winter provides root vegetables for the most warming and comforting soups of all. Spices enhance the wonderful tastes of the vegetables year round, and fresh herbs in spring and summer add qualities all their own. Whatever the season, soups can be highly nutritious as well as filling – full of vegetable protein, and rich in vitamins and minerals.

A blender or food processor is an extremely useful piece of equipment for making soups – it purées them in no time at all and with a minimum of effort. However, if you don't possess one, soups can be sieved to a smooth texture using a vegetable mill or a large wire sieve and a strong wooden spoon to push them through.

Vegetable stock cubes are easily obtainable, but if you prefer to make your own stock it is an excellent way of using up vegetable scraps. A home-made stock will make soups extra tasty too. There is a recipe on page 31.

LENTIL SOUP ♥

This is a real country soup, thick and warming. Adding three or four fried, sliced vegetarian sausages to this soup just before serving will turn it into a hearty main dish.

FOR 6–8

1¼ lb (550 g) green lentils, soaked for 2-3 hours	2 x 14 oz (400g) cans chopped tomatoes with juice
3½ pints (2 litres) water	2 tbs red wine (optional)
2 tsp sea salt	2 tbs fresh lemon juice
2 tbs olive oil	2 tbs brown sugar
1 large onion, chopped	2 tbs wine vinegar
2 stalks celery, chopped	freshly ground black pepper
3 carrots, sliced	chopped fresh thyme, oregano or basil, or chopped fresh tomatoes, to garnish
2 cloves garlic, crushed	

Put the lentils in a large pan and add the water. Bring to the boil, then cover and simmer for 20 minutes. Add the salt.

Meanwhile, heat the oil in another pan and cook the onion, celery, carrot and garlic gently, covered, for about 10 minutes or until soft.

Add the softened vegetables to the lentils and stir to mix. Add the tomatoes, wine, lemon juice, sugar and wine vinegar. Season with pepper. Bring to the boil, then leave to simmer gently, uncovered, for about 30 minutes or until the lentils are very tender. If the soup becomes too thick, add a little more water.

Check the seasoning and stir in chopped fresh herbs or tomatoes before serving.

POTATO AND CARROT SOUP ♥

A warming, comforting soup for cold weather. You can make it more substantial by sprinkling a few crisp browned vegetarian steak chunks over the top before serving – like nutritious croutons!

FOR 6

2 tbs olive oil	skimmed or soya milk to thin out
1 large onion, chopped	
2 large potatoes, peeled and diced	sea salt and freshly ground black pepper
8 large carrots, diced	chopped parsley to garnish
3 pints (1.75 litres) vegetable stock, or water and 3 vegetable stock cubes	

Heat the oil in a large pan and cook the onion gently, covered, until soft. Add the potatoes and carrots and stir well. Pour in the stock, bring to the boil and leave to cook over a low heat, partly covered, for 30–40 minutes or until all the vegetables are very soft and tender.

Purée three-quarters of the soup in a blender or food processor. Mix with the remainder of the soup and reheat briefly, thinning out with milk if required. Season to taste and serve hot, sprinkled with parsley.

TUSCAN BEAN AND CABBAGE SOUP ♥

This soup is nourishing and satisfying, and is delicious at any time of year, especially in cold weather. Serve with Italian bread such as ciabatta.

FOR 6

2 tbs olive oil

1 large onion, sliced

2 medium carrots, sliced thin

2 medium turnips, sliced thin

2-3 cloves garlic, crushed

12 oz (350g) cabbage, shredded

2 tbs chopped parsley

2 x 14 oz (400g) cans cannellini or butter beans, drained (or equivalent cooked dried, see page 185)

4 tomatoes, skinned (see page 59) and chopped, or 4 canned tomatoes

3½ pints (2 litres) vegetable stock

2 tbs finely chopped parsley to garnish

sea salt and freshly ground black pepper

finely grated cheese to hand around (optional)

Heat the oil in a large saucepan and cook the onion gently for 5 minutes, covered. Then add the carrots and turnips and stir until coated with oil. Stir in the garlic. Cook gently for 2–3 minutes.

Stir in the remaining ingredients and bring to the boil. Cover and simmer gently for 25 minutes or until the vegetables are tender. Season to taste, and add more stock if necessary. Serve sprinkled with chopped parsley, and provide a bowl of finely grated cheese to pass around for those who want it.

VEGETABLE SOUP ♥

I made this soup when invited by Pierre Franey of the New York Times to be his guest on his 'Great Cooks' series. It is warming winter food.

FOR 6–8

2 tbs olive oil

1 large onion, chopped

3 leeks, sliced thinly

1 clove garlic, crushed

1 head celery, chopped

4 large carrots, sliced

½ small white cabbage, shredded

12 oz (350g) new potatoes, cubed

1 tsp each chopped fresh thyme and rosemary

4 pints (2.25 litres) vegetable stock

8 medium tomatoes, skinned (see page 59) and chopped, or 1 x 14 oz (400g) can chopped tomatoes with their juice

1 tbs chopped fresh tarragon (optional)

sea salt and freshly ground black pepper

Heat the oil in a heavy saucepan and lightly brown the onion, leeks, garlic and celery for 5 minutes. Add the carrots, cabbage and potatoes and stir well. Stir in the thyme and rosemary. Cover with the stock and bring to the boil. Cover and leave to simmer until the vegetables are tender, stirring and testing occasionally.

Add the tomatoes and tarragon (if using) and stir them in. Season to taste and heat through. Serve with warm wholemeal rolls.

OPPOSITE: Tuscan Bean and Cabbage Soup

PARSNIP AND BUTTER BEAN SOUP

*W*onderful winter food, this soup is highly nutritious, very warming and full of flavour. Sweet parsnips make particularly delicious soups that are economical too.

FOR 4

2 tbs olive oil	*1½ pints (900 ml) vegetable stock*
1 large onion, chopped	
3 large cloves garlic, sliced	*1 bay leaf*
2 large parsnips, washed and chopped	*1 tbs fresh lemon juice*
	4 tbs crème fraîche or single cream
3 medium potatoes, washed and chopped	
	1 pint (600 ml) soya milk or skimmed milk
1 x 14 oz (400 g) can butter beans (or equivalent cooked dried, see page 185)	
	sea salt and freshly ground black pepper

Heat the oil in a heavy saucepan and stir in the onion and garlic. Cover and cook gently for 8–10 minutes or until softened. Add the chopped parsnips and potatoes and stir well, then add the butter beans with the juices from the can. Pour in the vegetable stock and add the bay leaf and lemon juice. Bring to the boil, then cover and leave to simmer very gently for 20–25 minutes or until the vegetables are completely softened.

Discard the bay leaf, then purée the soup in a blender or food processor, with the crème fraîche or single cream. Thin with the milk. Season to taste, and reheat gently for serving.

PUMPKIN SOUP ▾

*T*he vibrant colour of this soup – orange with small flecks of green – will cheer and warm on a chilly day. You can toast the pumpkin seeds and use them to garnish the soup (the shells of the seeds are edible although tough).

FOR 6

1¾ lb (800 g) piece of pumpkin, peeled, seeds and fibres removed and flesh cut into cubes	*2 tbs olive oil*
	2 onions, chopped
	1½ oz (40 g) parsley, chopped
	sea salt and freshly ground black pepper
2½ pints (1.5 litres) water	

In a large saucepan, simmer the pumpkin cubes in the water until they are very tender.

Meanwhile, heat the oil in a frying pan and sauté the onions until golden.

Purée the pumpkin and liquid in a blender or food processor, or press through a sieve, and return to the pan. Add the sautéed onions and the parsley. Season to taste and heat through.

OPPOSITE: Parsnip and Butter Bean Soup

RUSSIAN BORSCHT v

This famous soup from Russia is hearty and satisfying, a warming soup for winter weather. You can make a meal of it with some warm granary bread.

FOR 6

6 large beetroot, peeled	2 tbs fresh lemon juice
1 potato, peeled	sea salt and freshly ground black pepper
8oz (250g) green cabbage	
1 large onion, chopped finely	¼ pint (150ml) soured cream (optional)
2 tbs olive oil	
4oz (125g) tomatoes, skinned (see page 59) and chopped	chopped fresh dill or parsley to garnish
4 pints (2.25 litres) vegetable stock	

Slice the beetroot, potato and cabbage very finely, then cut the slices into matchsticks. Brown the onion lightly in the oil for 3–4 minutes, then add the rest of the vegetables and stir together for several minutes. Pour in enough stock to cover and bring to the boil. Simmer for 20–30 minutes or until tender.

Add the rest of the stock and the lemon juice. Purée half of the soup in a blender or food processor, then return it to the remaining soup in the pan and reheat gently. Season to taste. Put a dollop of soured cream on each bowl of soup (vegans can omit this) and garnish with chopped dill or parsley.

GREEN SOUP WITH PARSLEY v

The celery flavour in this soup is highlighted by the subtle taste of split peas. It is a deliciously wholesome soup, perfect for cold weather.

FOR 4

6oz (175g) dried split peas	1 bay leaf
2 tbs olive oil	1½ pints (900ml) vegetable stock
1 medium onion, chopped	
4 stalks celery, sliced	sea salt and freshly ground black pepper
2 carrots, sliced	
3 tbs chopped parsley	chopped parsley to garnish

Cover the split peas with hot water and leave to soak for 1 hour. Drain and set to one side.

Heat the oil in a large saucepan and sauté the onion for 3–4 minutes. Add the celery and carrots and cook over moderate heat until lightly browned. Add the drained split peas, the parsley and bay leaf. Pour in the stock and stir well. Cover the pan and bring to the boil, then leave to simmer for 1–1½ hours or until the split peas are very tender. Add more water or stock if needed as the soup cooks.

Season to taste and serve immediately, sprinkled with chopped parsley.

OPPOSITE: Russian Borscht

SWEETCORN CHOWDER

A great American classic, this creamy golden soup is easy to make and a treat at any time of the year. Its texture is as satisfying as its flavours.

FOR 4

1 very large potato or 2 small potatoes, peeled and cut into ½ inch (1.25 cm) cubes	¾ pint (450 ml) milk
¾ pint (450 ml) water	4 fl oz (125 ml) single cream
1 onion, chopped	sea salt and freshly ground black pepper
2 tbs olive oil	paprika to taste
1½ lb (700 g) fresh sweetcorn kernels, stripped from about 6 ears of sweetcorn (see page 34), or 2 x 14 oz (400 g) cans sweetcorn	pinch of dried thyme
	1 bay leaf
	freshly chopped parsley and chives, to taste

Parboil the potato in the water, salted, for 10 minutes. Meanwhile, cook the onion in the oil over a low heat, covered, for 5–8 minutes or until translucent. Add the onion to the potatoes with the remaining ingredients and bring back to the boil.

Leave to simmer for 20–30 minutes or until the sweetcorn is tender and the soup is slightly thickened, stirring occasionally. Discard the bay leaf before serving.

ASPARAGUS SOUP

The delicate flavour of asparagus comes through well in this attractive pale green soup. If fresh asparagus is not in season, substitute canned – the result will be just as delicious.

FOR 4

2 tbs vegetable oil	8 oz (250 g) fresh asparagus, tough ends of stalks removed, chopped, or equivalent canned asparagus, drained and chopped
1 onion, finely chopped	
1 medium potato, peeled and diced	
4 stalks celery, finely chopped	sea salt and freshly ground black pepper
1 pint (600 ml) vegetable stock	milk to thin the soup if necessary

In a large saucepan, heat the oil and cook the onion until soft and translucent. Add the potato and celery and cook for a further 2 minutes, stirring. Pour in half of the stock and bring to the boil, then cover and simmer for 10–15 minutes or until the potatoes are tender.

Add the asparagus and the remaining stock. Cover again and cook for 10 minutes or until all the vegetables are tender.

Ladle half of the vegetables into a blender or food processor and purée. Return to the pan and stir to mix with the remainder of the soup and vegetables. Season to taste and heat through. If the soup is too thick, thin with a little milk.

OPPOSITE: Sweetcorn Chowder

GARDEN SOUP WITH PESTO ❧

Utilizing the early summer vegetables from the garden makes this a light, refreshing soup. It is so pretty to look at, too, with the contrasting fresh greens and the orange of young carrot. Vegans can omit the garnish of grated cheese.

FOR 4–6

3 tbs olive oil	*6oz (175g) frozen peas, thawed*
1 clove garlic, crushed	
1 medium leek, sliced thinly	*1 small crisp lettuce, shredded*
2 large carrots, diced	*1 tbs chopped fresh tarragon*
1 small turnip, diced	*¼ pint (150ml) simple pesto sauce (see page 149)*
2 small potatoes, peeled and diced	
2 pints (1.2 litres) vegetable stock	*sea salt and freshly ground black pepper*
	grated cheese (optional)

Heat the olive oil in a large saucepan and sauté the garlic, leek, carrots, turnip and potatoes for 5–6 minutes or until beginning to soften. Pour in the stock and bring to the boil, then leave to simmer for 15–20 minutes or until the vegetables are tender.

Add the peas and lettuce and simmer for a further 5 minutes. Stir in the tarragon and pesto and season to taste. Serve with a bowl of freshly grated cheese to hand around.

COURGETTE AND WATERCRESS SOUP ❧

This lovely green soup has a distinctive, subtle flavour and is a treat served with hot garlic bread, or with croutons for a contrasting crunch. If you want a creamy, non-vegan version, add some crème fraîche or thick plain yogurt just before serving.

FOR 4–6

3 tbs olive oil	*2 bunches watercress, stalks trimmed*
2 Spanish onions, sliced finely	
2 pints (1.2 litres) vegetable stock	*sea salt and freshly ground black pepper*
2lb (1kg) courgettes, trimmed and chopped roughly	*fresh lemon juice*

Heat the oil in a heavy saucepan and stir in the sliced onions. Cover and cook them over a low heat for 10–15 minutes or until tender and sweet. Add the stock and bring to the boil, then add the courgettes. Simmer, uncovered, for 15 minutes or until they are very tender. Remove from the heat.

Add the watercress to the pan, stir well and cover. Leave to stand for 5 minutes.

Strain through a sieve set in a bowl. Set the liquid aside and purée the solids in a blender or food processor, or press them through a sieve, until perfectly smooth. Return them to the pan and stir in the liquid. Reheat the soup. Season to taste and add a little lemon juice to sharpen the flavour. Serve at once.

OPPOSITE: Garden Soup with Pesto

GAZPACHO ANDALUZ ♥

A wonderful chilled soup with refreshing tastes, full of natural vitamins. Serve in small bowls with the garnishes to hand around.

FOR 6

2 slices granary bread, crusts removed	2 canned pimientos, drained and chopped, or 1 large fresh red pepper, chopped
2 tbs olive oil	6 spring onions, chopped
3 tbs fresh lemon juice	½ cucumber, roughly chopped
3 cloves garlic, crushed	¾ pint (450 ml) tomato juice
1 x 1½ lb (750g) can tomatoes, or the same weight fresh tomatoes, skinned (see page 59) and chopped	sea salt and freshly ground black pepper
	2 tbs mayonnaise (optional)

For the garnish a selection from:

black olives	finely diced raw onion
finely diced cucumber	finely chopped tomatoes
chopped green pepper (or red or yellow)	finely chopped parsley
cubes of toasted or fried bread	

Soak the bread in the olive oil and lemon juice, with the garlic, while you prepare the vegetables.

Put everything, apart from the seasoning and mayonnaise, into the blender and run until smooth. Season to taste and stir in the mayonnaise, if using. Chill thoroughly before serving. Hand around the garnishes so that everyone adds their favourite.

SUMMERY TOMATO SOUP WITH DILL ♥

A fresh, summery soup, ideal served chilled for lunch on a warm day. Use home-grown tomatoes for the best flavour.

FOR 4–6

3 tbs olive oil	1 tsp ground allspice (optional)
2 large onions, sliced finely	pinch of sugar (optional)
2 large cloves garlic, crushed	sea salt and freshly ground black pepper
bunch of fresh dill, chopped	finely grated rind of ½ orange
3 pints (1.75 litres) vegetable stock	4 fl oz (125ml) soured cream (optional)
1 x 1½ lb (750g) can tomatoes, or the same weight fresh tomatoes, skinned (see page 59) and chopped	sprigs of fresh dill to garnish

Heat the oil in a saucepan and stir in the onions. Cover and cook gently for 10 minutes, stirring occasionally, until completely soft and sweet.

Add the garlic and cook, covered, for a further 5 minutes. Stir in half of the dill and cook, uncovered, for 3–4 minutes longer.

Pour in the vegetable stock and add the canned tomatoes with their juice or the chopped fresh tomatoes, the optional allspice and sugar. Season with salt and pepper. Bring to the boil and leave to simmer gently for 35–40 minutes.

Add the orange rind. Remove from the heat and allow to cool slightly. Purée the soup, in batches, in a blender or food processor until it is quite smooth. Add the remaining dill. Return it to the pan, unless serving cold, and heat through very gently for 5 minutes. Correct the seasoning and serve, with a dollop of soured cream on each serving, if you like, and garnished with a sprig of dill.

OPPOSITE: Gazpacho Andaluz

THICK ARTICHOKE SOUP

This simple soup has the most amazing flavour, and is a meal in itself with warm wholemeal rolls. Serve it with croutons too, if you want a contrasting crunch!

FOR 4

2 lb (1 kg) Jerusalem artichokes, peeled	*1 tbs olive oil*
2 pints (1.2 litres) vegetable stock	*5 tbs crème fraîche or single cream*
½ onion, finely chopped	*sea salt and freshly ground black pepper*

Put the artichokes in a saucepan, cover with cold water and bring to the boil. Cover and simmer until completely soft. Cool in the liquid, then drain.

Turn the artichokes into a blender or food processor, add half of the vegetable stock and blend until smooth, then gradually add the rest of the stock. Alternatively, press the artichokes through a sieve and stir in the stock.

Cook the onion in the oil until translucent. Meanwhile, reheat the soup.

Stir the onion and crème fraîche or single cream into the hot soup and season to taste.

CROUTONS ⌄

Add lovely munchy croutons to soups for extra texture or for a more filling meal. Using the optional garlic makes the croutons even tastier.

FOR 4

4 medium slices bread, crusts removed	*1 large clove garlic, crushed (optional)*
vegetable oil for frying	

Cut the crustless slices of bread into tiny cubes. Heat the oil gently in a frying pan and fry the bread over a medium heat, shaking to turn them until they begin to turn golden and become crisp. Add the garlic, if using, towards the end of cooking, keeping the heat down to prevent the garlic from burning. Stir the garlic croutons thoroughly.

When evenly browned – and be careful not to overcook them – remove the croutons from the pan with a slotted spoon and drain on kitchen paper.

Keep in a very low oven until ready to use.

VEGETABLE STOCK v

This is the basis of many soups. It can be made whenever you have vegetable scraps or peelings to hand and then stored in the refrigerator. It is worth getting into the habit of making vegetable stock regularly, so that you always have some when you need it.

MAKES – as much as you like!

vegetable scraps, such as	*sea salt*
onion, carrot, leek, cabbage,	*black peppercorns*
tomato, broccoli, cauliflower,	*bay leaves*
Jerusalem artichoke, potato	*fresh herbs in season or dried*
peelings	*herbs*
cold water to cover	

Put the vegetable scraps or trimmings into a large saucepan and cover with cold water. Add a little sea salt, a sprinkling of black peppercorns and a couple of bay leaves for flavour. Add a small bunch of fresh herbs – such as sage, parsley, thyme, chives and/or tarragon – according to season, or a tablespoon or so of dried mixed herbs.

Bring to the boil and simmer, covered, for 45 minutes. Then leave to stand until cold.

Strain, and store in the refrigerator for up to 5 days.

DUMPLINGS v

Dumplings are a mainstay of the family cook, and they always WERE meatless, although of course you need to use vegetable suet to make them vegetarian. Simply cook them in simmering vegetable stock (above) and serve them with any of your favourite meatless meals. You can also make them using wholemeal flour, or half white and half wholemeal.

MAKES 8

4oz (125g) plain flour	*sea salt and freshly ground*
2oz (50g) vegetable suet	*black pepper*

Mix the flour with the suet and some salt and pepper, then add enough cold water to mix to an elastic dough. Shape into 8 dumplings and cook in simmering stock for 20–25 minutes.

VARIATIONS

To the basic mixture add one of the following:
- 1 tbs each grated Parmesan cheese and chopped parsley
- 1 tbs dried mixed herbs
- 1 tbs each grated cheese and chopped fresh chives
- 1 tbs chopped fresh basil
- 1 tbs grated cheese

CHAPTER TWO

Light Meals and Side Dishes

Within this section you'll find an exciting range of snacks, starters and side dishes that you can make quickly and easily – from tempting nibbles to go with a drink before a meal, such as crisp and succulent cheese palmiers, to classic dishes like vegetable tempura, which always looks so amazing on the plate and is loved by everybody.

The selection of Mexican recipes here demonstrates the versatility of the tortilla, the Mexican pancake, which is used in tacos, enchiladas, burritos and nachos. All of these make wonderful and satisfying quick meals. They are highly nutritious because they often contain refried beans or vegetarian mince, as well as good supplies of carbohydrates. Lightly spiced with chilli, these irresistible dishes deserve to become part of every family cook's repertoire. Most of the special ingredients needed for preparing Mexican recipes – tortillas, taco sauces, canned mild chillies and refried beans – are now available at big supermarkets. They are a welcome addition to the range of ethnic foods we can enjoy and explore.

MEXICAN SNACK FOODS

THE VERSATILE TORTILLA

Tortillas are the Mexican version of pancakes, made of wheat flour or corn (maize). They are the basis of tacos, burritos, enchiladas, nachos and quesadillas. You can buy tortillas ready-made.

Tacos are corn tortillas folded in half and fried crisp. You can buy tacos, or you can make your own tortilla shells by frying tortillas, using a ladle to make a hollow in the centre (see page 35). Use your imagination and any fillings inspired by favourite recipes in this book to make wonderful snacks. For authentic Mexican flavour add canned mild chillies to your mixture – they will not blow your head off as fresh chillies are apt to do!

BURRITOS AND CHIMICHANGAS

A burrito is a warm wheat-flour tortilla filled with cooked vegetables (often including beans or refried beans), made into a parcel and topped with salad. Courgettes, broccoli, mangetout, carrots and spinach all make excellent fillings and go well with the grated cheese.

Put the filling of cooked vegetables, beans, grated cheese and shredded salad into the centre of the warm tortilla, fold the bottom quarter over, then the sides, then the top, to make an 'envelope'. Serve immediately.

For a 'Chimichanga' simply fry the filled burrito in shallow oil until golden brown. Serve with a Mexican salsa (for home-made versions, see page 152), guacamole (page 157) or soured cream.

QUESADILLAS

A quesadilla is a turnover, made with a wheat-flour tortilla and fried lightly in oil. Here refried beans and cheese provide the filling.

FOR 1 (Makes 2)

2 small wheat-flour tortillas	*2 tbs bottled taco sauce or home-made salsa (see page 152)*
2 tbs canned refried beans, thinned out with a little water	
2 oz (50g) cheese, sliced thinly	*sliced fresh chilli (optional)*
	vegetable oil for frying

Spread the tortillas with the refried bean mixture and place the sliced cheese on top. Dot the taco sauce or salsa on the cheese and add a slice or two of fresh chilli if you like things spicy-hot!

Fold the tortillas into half-moon shapes and fry in a very little oil in a hot pan until browned on both sides and heated through. Eat immediately.

NACHOS

These are just brilliant! If your family is hungry and looking for a very fast snack, make these nibbles instead of opening a packet of potato crisps.

FOR 6–8

5 oz (150g) tortilla chips	*6 tbs bottled hot taco sauce (optional)*
8 oz (250g) mild Cheddar cheese, grated	

Spread the tortilla chips one layer deep in shallow baking dishes. Sprinkle with the cheese and dot the optional sauce on top. Bake at 200°C/400°F/gas 6 for 5 minutes. Serve immediately and eat at once!

MEXICAN CORN BREAD

This is nothing less than beautiful – spicy, cheesy and very more-ish! Serve it warm from the oven, or reheat slices in a microwave for 30 seconds (this will retain its tender crumb and moistness).

FOR 4–6

1 free-range egg	4 fl oz (125 ml) crème fraîche or soured cream
2 tbs olive oil	
½ oz (15 g) fresh green chillies, chopped very finely	4 oz (125 g) yellow cornmeal (polenta)
6 oz (175 g) canned sweetcorn, drained, or 2-3 fresh ears of sweetcorn, kernels stripped off	1 tsp sea salt
	1 tsp baking powder
	8 oz (250 g) Cheddar cheese, grated

Beat the egg with the oil until blended. Add the chillies. Stir in the sweetcorn, crème fraîche, cornmeal, salt, baking powder and all but 2 oz (50 g) of the cheese. Pour into an 8–9 inch (20–22.5 cm) shallow cake tin. Sprinkle the remaining cheese over the top.

Bake at 180°C/350°F/gas 4 for 40 minutes. Cool slightly in the tin, then turn out and serve warm.

Stripping Corn Kernels off the Cob

Remove the outer leaves or husks and all silk from the corn. Holding the corn cob upright with the flat end firmly on a board, run a sharp knife down the length, between the kernels and the cob, to strip the kernels away.

TACOS WITH TOMATOES AND VEGETARIAN MINCE ♥

This is a really tasty snack meal, with its appetizing mixture of textures, flavours and colours. Vegans can make these omitting the cheese topping.

MAKES 8

12 oz (350 g) vegetarian mince	sea salt and freshly ground black pepper
2 tbs olive oil	
2 oz (50 g) almonds, chopped	1-2 tsp cayenne pepper or to taste
2 small onions, sliced finely	
2 cloves garlic, sliced finely	8 taco shells, warmed
3 tomatoes, skinned (see page 59) and chopped (fresh or canned)	3 oz (75 g) Cheddar cheese, grated (optional)
	shredded lettuce
a little tomato juice to bind	

Brown the vegetarian mince in 1 tbs oil for 3–4 minutes, then add the almonds and cook until they are browned too. In a separate pan, soften the onions and garlic in the rest of the oil. Stir in the tomatoes and juice and cook until well amalgamated. Season to taste with salt, pepper and cayenne. Add the mince and almond mixture and stir well.

Fill the warm taco shells. Top with grated cheese and shredded lettuce. Serve with the no-cook salsa or the chilli sauce on page 152.

SPICY REFRIED BEAN TACOS ♥

*R*ich and filling, a snack meal for the hungry! Crisp taco shells are filled with a spicy tomato and bean mixture, shredded lettuce and grated cheese, and topped with avocado slices and soured cream. (Vegans can omit the cheese and soured cream.)

MAKES 4

8oz (250g) canned refried beans	*4 spring onions, sliced finely*
2 tbs bottled taco sauce or home-made salsa (see page 152)	*1-2 tsp hot chilli relish or to taste*
	sea salt
4 medium tomatoes, skinned (see page 59) and chopped	*4 taco shells, warmed*
	grated cheese (optional)
	shredded lettuce

To garnish:

sliced avocado	*soured cream (optional)*

Heat the refried beans with the taco sauce or salsa. Add the chopped tomatoes and mash thoroughly. Add the spring onions and cook gently for 4–5 minutes, stirring frequently. Season to taste with chilli relish and a little salt if liked.

Half-fill the warm taco shells with the mixture and top with grated cheese and shredded lettuce (you can put the lettuce at the bottom of the shell if you prefer). Garnish with a slice or two of avocado and a dollop of soured cream.

BEAN TACOS WITH RED PEPPERS ♥

*M*emorable tastes which linger on the palate and make a snack meal with a difference. As with the other tacos, vegans can eat these if they omit the cheese and soured cream.

MAKES 8

1 tbs olive oil	*4 tbs chilli sauce*
1 onion, sliced	*1 lettuce, shredded*
1 red pepper, deseeded and chopped	*8 taco shells, warmed*
1 x 14oz (400g) can pinto or kidney beans, drained (or equivalent cooked dried beans, see page 185)	*3oz (75g) Cheddar cheese, grated*
	soured cream

Heat the oil and soften the onion and red pepper for 5 minutes. Add the beans and cook uncovered for 10 minutes. Mash, and then mix in the chilli sauce.

Put shredded lettuce into the warm taco shells, spoon the warm bean mixture over the top, and top with cheese and soured cream.

Tortilla shells

Deep fry a corn tortilla in very hot oil, pushing the centre down with a ladle. Cook until golden – half a minute or so. Remove the ladle and allow the tortilla to finish cooking until golden. Drain on kitchen paper and dry. Fill the central hollow with any of the fillings above, top with grated cheese and finish with shredded salad.

NEXT SPREAD: A Mexican feast with, left to right, Soured Cream Enchiladas with Tomato and Chilli Salsa (see page 152) on the side, Corn Bread, Tortillas piled with mixed vegetables, and Guacamole (see page 157)

ENCHILADAS

*E*nchiladas are the Mexican equivalent to our stuffed pancake – wheat-flour
tortillas are rolled up around a tasty filling and then baked, often topped with
a spicy sauce.

TRADITIONAL ENCHILADAS

A tasty dish that is highly nutritious. The creamy vegetarian mince filling is rolled up inside tortillas which are baked until crisp. Serve a salad of crisp green leaves and orange segments alongside, for a refreshing contrast.

MAKES 4

8oz (250g) vegetarian mince	*4 fl oz (125ml) crème fraîche*
2 tbs vegetable oil	*or soured cream*
½ small onion, chopped finely	*¼–½ tsp chilli powder*
4oz (125g) cheese, grated	*4 wheat-flour tortillas*

Sauté the vegetarian mince in the oil. Mix with the onion, cheese, crème fraîche and chilli powder and use to fill the tortillas. Roll them up and bake seam-side down at 180°C/350°F/gas 4 for 10–12 minutes or until hot through and crisp on top.

Chillies

Chillies come from a large botanical family with many varieties. You see them in the shops in all sizes and colours – red, green, cream and even purple. The plump green jalapeño chilli is popular and used in many Mexican dishes. Chillies vary in strength quite considerably so it is prudent to err on the side of caution when adding them to your recipe: start with a little and then add to taste.

Dried chillies are a useful standby in the kitchen cupboard, and can be very hot. Canned chillies, however, tend to be milder and are a truly delicious way of spicing. Beware of chillies in vinegar – they blow your head off.

SOURED CREAM ENCHILADAS

These are rich and succulent, and make a brilliant dish for a casual summer meal with friends, served with a tossed salad. To make the meal more substantial, add Mexican rice 'n' beans or Spanish rice (see page 97).

MAKES 6

6 wheat-flour tortillas	*4oz (125g) cheese, grated finely*
3 tbs salsa (see page 152) or light tomato sauce (see page 151)	*½ pint (300ml) soured cream*
4oz (125g) chopped onion	*olives to garnish*

Brush the surface of each tortilla with some salsa or tomato sauce. Mix the chopped onion with the grated cheese and half of the soured cream. Put this filling into the centre of the tortillas and roll them up. Place seam-side down in a baking dish. Cover with the rest of the soured cream, and bake at 190°C/375°F/gas 5 for 20 minutes or until golden.

Garnish with olives and hand more salsa or tomato sauce around for those who want it.

CHEESE ENCHILADAS

This is a wonderfully simple snack meal, or it can be a light supper served with rice and a tossed salad such as the watercress salad with garlic croutons on page 30 or the carrot salad on page 134.

MAKES 6

2 tbs sweetcorn relish	*4 canned tomatoes, drained and chopped*
4oz (125g) Cheddar cheese, grated	*3 spring onions, chopped*
2oz (50g) shredded iceberg lettuce	*6 wheat-flour tortillas*
	6 tbs soured cream (optional)

Mix together the relish, cheese, lettuce, tomatoes and spring onions and roll up inside the tortillas. Bake seam-side down at 190°C/375°F/gas 5 for 20 minutes or until the tops of the tortillas are crisp and lightly browned. Top with soured cream, if using.

MELTING AUBERGINES WITH SWEET PEPPERS

This makes an excellent light lunch or supper dish, or you can serve it as a starter for a more formal meal. A glass of red wine and crusty wholemeal bread will complete the menu.

FOR 4

2 medium aubergines, cut into thick slices	8oz (250g) soft goat's cheese or any soft cheese, sliced
sea salt	freshly ground black pepper
3 tbs olive oil	stoned olives to garnish
2 canned pimientos, drained and each cut into 4 pieces, or 1 large fresh red pepper, quartered and skinned (see page 59)	

Sprinkle the slices of aubergine with a touch of salt. Brush them with olive oil and place on a large baking tray. Bake at 220°C/425°F/gas 7 for 10–12 minutes or until soft and golden brown.

Layer the aubergine slices, pimientos and goat's cheese in four or eight stacks on a baking tray, seasoning with freshly ground black pepper as you go along. Top each stack with a piece of cheese. Return to the oven and bake for 5 minutes to heat through. Garnish with a stoned olive or two, and serve immediately.

AUBERGINE CAVIAR ˅

This Middle Eastern dip is also known as 'poor man's caviar', although it is just as luxurious as the real thing. Serve with toasted triangles of pitta bread or carrot sticks.

FOR 4

2 large aubergines	1 large clove garlic, crushed
juice of 2-3 lemons	sea salt
2½ tbs tahini (sesame paste)	4 tbs chopped parsley
3 tbs sesame seeds	1 tbs olive oil

Pierce the aubergines several times with a sharp knife. Bake at 190°C/375°F/gas 5 for 30–40 minutes or until soft. Set aside to cool for about 30 minutes.

Peel the aubergines and discard the skin. Put the flesh in a bowl and immediately add the lemon juice. Mash well, or blend in the food processor. Add the tahini, sesame seeds and garlic and mix in thoroughly. Season with salt.

Spoon into a serving dish, cover and chill. Before serving, sprinkle with the parsley and drizzle the olive oil over the top.

OPPOSITE: Melting Aubergines with Sweet Peppers

LIGHT VEGETABLE TEMPURA

This tempura from Japan makes one of the best snack meals in the world. Lovely with a sweet and sour sauce (see page 153), the chilli sauce on page 152, or the tamari sauce here, and served with boiled rice.

FOR 4

8oz (250g) courgettes, sliced thickly	For the batter:
	4oz (125g) plain flour
8oz (250g) small button mushrooms	*1 free-range egg*
	7 fl oz (200ml) water
8oz (250g) broccoli florets	*large pinch of sea salt*
4oz (125g) cauliflower florets	Optional sauce:
vegetable oil for deep frying	*4 tbs tamari sauce*
	grated fresh ginger and spring onion to taste

Prepare the vegetables. Put the batter ingredients into the blender or food processor and run it until smooth. It is ready to use.

Make the sauce you intend to use. Set aside.

Pour the oil about 3 inches (7.5 cm) deep into a large saucepan. Heat to 170°C/325°F.

Dip the pieces of vegetable into the batter one at a time and place carefully in the hot oil. Do not fry too many pieces at once. Fry the vegetables, turning them over occasionally, until they are lightly golden all over – each batch takes a couple of minutes. Lift out and put on to kitchen paper to drain. Keep these pieces hot in a warm oven while you fry the next batch. When all are fried, serve without delay.

COURGETTES WITH SWEETCORN ♥

This simple recipe is easily prepared, and its colours are delightful – yellow and green glow off the plate. Try it with saffron rice (see page 94) or with plain noodles and a tossed salad.

FOR 3–4

2 tbs olive oil	*small handful of fresh tarragon, chopped, or 1 tbs dried tarragon*
1 lb (500g) courgettes, cubed	
12 oz (350g) canned sweetcorn, drained	*sea salt and freshly ground black pepper*
1 small onion, chopped	
1 large clove garlic, crushed	

Heat the oil in a large frying pan and add all the ingredients. Cook gently, stirring, for 5 minutes or until they begin to soften. Then cover with a lid and cook over a very low heat for a further 5 minutes. Check the seasoning and serve hot.

OPPOSITE: Light Vegetable Tempura with Chilli Sauce

ASPARAGUS WITH GARLIC

When asparagus is in season, make the most of it and try this unusual way of serving it, with garlic-flavoured oil, lemon juice and freshly grated Parmesan.

FOR 4

2-3 cloves garlic, crushed	4-6 tbs finely grated
4 tbs olive oil	Parmesan cheese
2lb (1kg) asparagus	2 tsp fresh lemon juice

Mix crushed garlic to taste with the oil and set aside. Stand the asparagus spears upright in a tall pan of boiling water (the tips should not be submerged), cover and cook for 8–10 minutes or until tender. Lift the asparagus carefully into a colander to drain.

Arrange the asparagus on warm plates and spoon the garlic oil over the tips. Sprinkle with Parmesan and lemon juice, and serve immediately, with warm crusty bread to mop up the juices.

LEMON GREEN BEANS ⌄

With grilled tomatoes and pitta bread, this fresh-tasting vegetable dish will make a lovely light meal. Or you can serve it to accompany a main dish such as the baked sweetcorn pudding on page 60.

FOR 3–4

8oz (250g) fine green beans	sea salt and freshly ground
2oz (50g) margarine	black pepper
3 tbs fresh lemon juice	3 tbs chopped parsley

Steam the beans for 3–4 minutes or until slightly softened. Melt the margarine in a pan and stir in the beans. Cover and cook over moderately low heat for about 5 minutes or until tender.

Add the lemon juice and season to taste. Cook for a further 3 minutes, then sprinkle on the parsley. Mix well, and put into a serving dish.

Steaming

Cooking vegetables in a steamer conserves their valuable vitamins and minerals, and retains their full flavour. Vegetables can be steamed either whole, sliced or chopped. Time allowed depends on the size and type of vegetable, and whether you wish to cook them to softness or 'al dente' (slightly crisp). Steamers can be bought at all good kitchen shops.

Cooking vegetables in a microwave oven is also in effect steaming them: covered with film wrap, and with a little water added, this method also brings out the full flavour of the vegetables whilst retaining their goodness.

OPPOSITE: Asparagus with Garlic (top) and Lemon Green Beans

VEGETABLE PURÉES

*Y*ou can adapt this basic recipe that uses broccoli to make many other vegetable purées, such as carrot, Brussels sprout, cauliflower, courgette, pumpkin, potato with celeriac, parsnip, cabbage and swede. Two other variations are suggested right.

FOR 6

2 lb (1kg) broccoli, trimmed and chopped	*2 oz (50g) cheese, grated*
¼ pint (150 ml) crème fraîche or single cream	*½ tsp each grated nutmeg and freshly ground black pepper*
2 tbs soured cream	*sea salt*

Steam the broccoli for 8–10 minutes or until tender. Put it into a food processor with the crème fraîche or single cream and purée thoroughly, or press through a sieve. Stir in the soured cream and grated cheese. Add the nutmeg and pepper, and salt to taste.

LEEK AND POTATO PURÉE: Cook 1½ lb (750 g) potatoes, peeled, and 6 large leeks, sliced, in separate pans of boiling salted water until tender. Drain well, reserving the cooking liquid from the leeks. Soften 2 cloves garlic, sliced finely, in 3 tbs olive oil; add the leeks and cook gently for 10 minutes. Meanwhile, purée the potatoes in a blender or food processor with ¼ pint (150 ml) crème fraîche or single cream (vegans can use tofu instead). Add the leek and garlic mixture and run the machine again until the purée is completely smooth, adding some of the reserved leek cooking liquid to thin to the desired consistency. Season to taste, and reheat gently before serving.

CREAMED SPINACH PURÉE: Steam 2 lb (1 kg) fresh spinach, trimmed, until tender, then drain well, pressing out all excess liquid. Chop the spinach finely or work in a food processor until quite fine. Heat 1 tbs butter or olive oil in a pan, add the spinach and heat through, stirring. Stir in ¼ pint (150 ml) crème fraîche or single cream. Season to taste and serve.

CHEESE AND NUT PÂTÉ

*C*runchy and garlicky, this pâté makes a great start to a meal, or a light lunch in its own right with a tossed salad, such as the special rocket salad on page 129.

FOR 4

1 slice wholemeal bread, crusts removed	*3 oz (75 g) Cheshire cheese, grated*
3 fl oz (75 ml) skimmed milk or soya milk	*1 large clove garlic, crushed*
5 oz (150 g) walnut pieces or pecans	*2 tbs olive oil*
	freshly ground black pepper
	sprigs of parsley to garnish

Soak the bread in the milk. Blend the nuts roughly in a food processor – not too smooth because you want the pâté to have texture. With a fork, work the nuts, cheese, garlic and oil into the soaked bread. Season with lots of pepper. Press into a mould or terrine, and chill.

To serve, turn out and garnish with sprigs of parsley. Eat with thin toast or baby tomatoes, celery and carrot sticks and a selection of other crudités in season.

BELOW: Cheese and Nut Pâté

CHEESE PALMIERS

These light cheese-filled pastries just melt in the mouth. Perfect as an appetizer to nibble before a meal, you will find that they disappear like the melting snow.

MAKES 20

8oz (250g) frozen or home-made puff pastry (see page 178)

8oz (250g) Cheddar cheese, grated

paprika

Roll out the pastry thinly into an oblong. Cover thickly with the cheese and press it down well. Sprinkle generously with paprika.

Fold one long edge of the pastry into the centre. Moisten the upper side of the edge with water. Fold the other long edge into the centre and press down to seal the edges together. Cut across into ¼ inch (0.5 cm) slices. Lay them, cut-side down, on a well-greased baking tray.

Bake at 220°C/425°F/gas 7 for 20 minutes or until golden brown. Cool on a wire rack for 5 minutes, and they are ready to serve.

FILO CHEESE STRAWS

These 'cigars' are a variation on the theme of cheese straws, and they really are irresistible, so you probably need to make more than you expect! Use a cheese with a good, strong flavour.

MAKES 12–14

4oz (125g) filo pastry

olive oil

6oz (175g) cheese, finely grated

freshly ground black pepper

Cut the filo sheets in half crosswise. Brush each one with olive oil, then fold in half and brush with oil again. Place a narrow band of grated cheese along one long edge and grind black pepper over the top. Roll up tightly. Cut the roll in half and brush the top with olive oil. Repeat with the remaining filo sheets. Place on a greased baking sheet and bake at 220°C/425°F/gas 7 for 15 minutes. Eat hot, or while still warm from the oven.

LIGHT SAUSAGE ROLLS ⱽ

These are so satisfying that any would-be meat eaters will love them! The first version wraps the vegetarian sausages in puff pastry, while the second uses crisp filo pastry. Vegans can omit the egg yolk coating and cheese.

MAKES 8

8 large vegetarian sausages	*1 free-range egg yolk, beaten*
8 oz (250 g) frozen or home-made puff pastry (see page 178)	

Grill or fry the vegetarian sausages as instructed on the packaging. Leave to cool.

Roll out the pastry fairly thinly and cut into eight rectangles that are the length of the sausages. Roll up a sausage in each rectangle so that the pastry just overlaps, and put seam-side down on a greased baking sheet. Score the top with a sharp knife, making long diagonal lines. Brush with beaten egg yolk and bake at 200°C/400°F/gas 6 for 25 minutes or until the pastry is puffed and golden.

MAKES 8

8 small vegetarian sausages	*8 slivers firm cheese*
8 sheets filo pastry	
olive oil	

Grill or fry the vegetarian sausages as instructed on the packaging. Leave to cool.

Cut each sheet of filo pastry in half. Brush the pieces of filo with olive oil and fold each one in half. Brush with oil again. Roll up a sausage and a sliver of cheese in a folded piece of filo, then roll up each roll in the remaining folded pieces of filo. Brush the tops of the rolls with more olive oil and place on a greased baking sheet. Bake at 200°C/400°F/gas 6 for 20 minutes or until golden.

PARTY EGGS

You can vary the flavours in this recipe by using different relishes – sweetcorn or tomato for example – and curry powder instead of paprika. Feel free to improvise!

FOR 6

6 free-range eggs	*sea salt and freshly ground black pepper*
5 tbs bottled or home-made mayonnaise (see page 150)	*paprika*
1 tsp mild mustard or more to taste	*To garnish:*
2 tbs sweet cucumber relish (optional)	*stoned olives, sliced, or capers*
	sprigs of parsley

Hard-boil the eggs for 10 minutes. Drain the eggs and plunge into cold water. Leave to cool.

When the eggs are cold, peel them carefully. Cut in half lengthwise and scoop out the yolks into a bowl. Mash the yolks with the mayonnaise, mustard, and relish if using. Season to taste with salt, pepper and paprika.

Pile the mixture back into the egg whites. Arrange on a plate and garnish with olives or capers and sprigs of parsley.

CRISP FILO MUSHROOM PARCELS v

*I*rresistible morsels, these are little mush-rooms wrapped up in filo pastry and cooked until crisp and golden. Eat them freshly made, on cocktail sticks if you are offering them as a nibble to go with drinks.

MAKES 24

7oz (200g) filo pastry	24 tiny button mushrooms
olive oil	

Leave the sheets of filo pastry stacked. Cut the stack into 4 inch (10 cm) squares, then separate them; you need 24 squares. Brush each square with olive oil and place a tiny mushroom in the centre. Fold the filo around the mushroom to make a parcel. Brush the outside with more olive oil.

Bake on a metal baking sheet at 200°C/400°F/gas 6 for 20 minutes or until crisp and golden. Leave to cool for at least 5 minutes before serving.

MUSHROOM TRIANGLES

*C*risp golden brown parcels of filo pastry contain a creamy mushroom mixture that is flavoured with garlic and fresh herbs.

MAKES 4

2 tbs olive oil	1 oz (30g) cornflour
3½ oz (100g) shallots, chopped	2 tbs chopped fresh basil or
2-3 cloves garlic, crushed	tarragon
8oz (250g) mushrooms, sliced	sea salt and freshly ground
2 tbs dry white wine	black pepper
7 fl oz (200ml) double cream	4 sheets filo pastry
7 fl oz (200ml) milk	melted butter
	beaten egg to glaze

Heat the oil in a large saucepan and cook the shallots gently, covered, for 5 minutes or until soft. Add the garlic and mushrooms and cook for a further 8–10 minutes, uncovered and stirring occasionally. Add the wine and boil until it has evaporated, then stir in the cream. Bring to the boil and boil gently for 5 minutes.

Mix the milk with the cornflour, then add to the pan and bring back to the boil, stirring well. The mixture should be very thick. Remove from the heat and stir in the basil or tarragon. Season to taste. Leave to cool.

Cut one sheet of filo in half lengthways. Brush one filo strip with melted butter and set the other strip on top. Brush with butter again. Spoon one-quarter of the mushroom mixture on to one end of the layered filo strip. Bring one corner up over the filling and press it on to the opposite side of the strip, to make a diagonal fold. Press the edges together to seal. Flip this triangle shape up on the pastry strip. Continue flipping the triangle over and over, to the end of the strip. Fill and shape three more triangles in the same way.

Put the mushroom triangles on a baking sheet and brush them with beaten egg. Bake at 220°C/425°F/gas 7 for 8–10 minutes or until the pastry is crisp and golden brown. Serve warm.

OPPOSITE: Crisp Filo Mushroom Parcels, served with Light Tomato Sauce (see page 151) and American Soured Cream Dip (see page 156)

JUICES

*V*egetable and fruit juices are not only delicious, they are renowned for their health-giving qualities. They are full of flavour as well as being packed with minerals and vitamins. These nutrients are absorbed very quickly into the body, and have a fast revitalizing effect. Complementary practitioners use juices in the treatment of numerous specific ailments and diseases.

Regular intake of vegetable and fruit juices maintains vitality and general good health. They are best drunk as fresh as possible, although you can keep them for several hours in an airtight jar in the fridge. For best results use a good electric juicer – juicing by hand to produce more than a small glassful can be exhausting, and is impossible for most vegetables.

FRUIT JUICES ❧

*T*hese are deliciously refreshing at any time of year, and always best when the fruit is in full season. Try squeezed juices: orange, grapefruit, lemon and tangerine; or juices extracted in an electric juicer: apple, apricot, blackberry, blueberry, blackcurrant, grape, kiwi, mango, melon, pineapple, pear, peach, papaya, plum, raspberry, strawberry. You can mash banana and add it to the above.

Some aromatic mixtures are:

banana and peach	mango and orange
banana and berries	peach and apricot
banana and apple	pineapple and peach
pear and apple	grape and apple

Or you can mix fruit and vegetable juices. The variety is endless, and you will enjoy trying out all the different combinations possible as the seasons turn. Some suggested combinations are:

carrot and apple	cucumber and peach
apple and celery	cucumber and apple
carrot and orange	celery and pineapple

VEGETABLE JUICES ❧

*C*arrot, tomato and cucumber juices are very pleasant drunk straight. If you prefer you can mix them with a small amount of strong-tasting juices such as spinach, lettuce, cabbage, celery, beetroot, parsley or watercress, which are too strong to drink on their own in any quantity.

You can make excellent 'juice cocktails'. Serve them on ice garnished with fresh herbs.

Here are some delicious combinations:
carrot, beetroot and cucumber
carrot and cucumber
cabbage, celery and tomato
tomato and alfalfa sprouts
carrot, celery, tomato, pepper, spinach and beetroot
with a touch of parsley and watercress

OPPOSITE: (left to right) In the bottles: beetroot, orange; in the box, back row: red grape and apple, carrot, pink grapefruit; front row: peach, cucumber and apple, papaya; front of picture: fresh tomato

CHAPTER THREE

Main Courses

Among the delights of cooking with vegetables is the huge variety of dishes that you can make. When it comes to the main part of the meal, though, some people still feel that a vegetarian dish is not as substantial as one that contains meat. So to satisfy that need, which also extends to people who are trying to give up meat and finding that they miss it, food technology has come up with some delicious vegetable-based alternatives.

The quality of 'TVP', or textured vegetable protein, has come a long, long way since the early days when it was, frankly, almost inedible. Today's TVP is excellent, and is available as mince, chunks, sausages and burgers. It is highly nutritious, too, containing 32g protein per 100g. For notes on how to use meat substitutes, see page 186.

Meat substitutes can be added to most of the recipes in this chapter, but, if you don't like them, you can omit them from the recipes, adding more vegetables as an alternative. In the same way, you can leave out onions and celery if you don't like them, increasing other vegetables that you do like. Interpret the recipes to suit your tastes and those of your family.

CHILLI NON CARNE ♥

*T*he classic chilli con carne – made with vegetarian mince instead of meat! It can be served either with rice or with baked potatoes, and a tossed salad of your choice. Mexican corn bread (see page 34) is another delicious accompaniment.

FOR 4

2 tbs olive oil	*1 x 14oz (400g) can red kidney beans, drained*
1 large onion, sliced finely	
2 cloves garlic, crushed	*1-2 canned mild green chillies, drained and chopped (optional)*
1½ tsp chilli powder or to taste	
8oz (250g) vegetarian mince	*sea salt*
¾ pint (450ml) vegetable stock	
1 x 14oz (400g) can chopped tomatoes	

Heat the oil and sauté the onion for 3–4 minutes, then add the garlic, chilli powder and mince and stir until well mixed. Brown for 5 minutes, stirring. Add the stock and the tomatoes with their juice, then leave to simmer gently, covered, for 20 minutes.

Add the kidney beans and the optional chilli and simmer for a further 15 minutes.

Season to taste with a little salt if necessary, and leave to stand for 10 minutes before serving to allow the flavours to develop.

TASTY BEANBURGERS

*S*o quick and easy to prepare, these beanburgers make a scrumptious lunch. Put a little chopped salad or a slice of cheese inside each bap, and serve with grilled tomatoes and the green bean salad on page 141.

MAKES 4

2 tbs olive oil plus more for frying burgers	*2oz (50g) fresh breadcrumbs*
	1 free-range egg
1 onion, chopped finely	*pinch of chilli powder*
2 cloves garlic, sliced finely	*sea salt and freshly ground black pepper*
1 tsp cumin seeds (optional)	
2 tbs chopped parsley	*warm baps to serve*
1 x 14oz (400g) can black-eyed or cannellini beans, drained	

Heat the oil and soften the onion and garlic, covered, for 5–6 minutes. Add the cumin seeds and cook for a further 3 minutes. Off the heat stir in the parsley and the beans. Mash until smooth, or blend in the food processor. Stir in the breadcrumbs and then the egg, mixing thoroughly. Season to taste with chilli powder, salt and pepper.

Shape into four burgers and fry in hot, shallow olive oil for 3–4 minutes on each side or until lightly browned. Serve inside warm fresh baps, with a little chopped salad or a slice of cheese.

STIR-FRY OF SPRING VEGETABLES WITH NOODLES ▾

A quick supper dish, with fresh flavours and appetizing spicing. Stir-fries make healthy, nutritious meals which you can vary widely, using different vegetables and herbs in season. Vegans can make this using plain noodles.

FOR 4

3 spring onions, sliced finely	*3 tbs soy sauce*
½ inch (1cm) root ginger, peeled and grated finely	*1 tbs black bean sauce*
2 cloves garlic, sliced finely	*2 tbs dark sesame oil*
3oz (75g) French beans	*8oz (250g) Chinese egg noodles, cooked and drained (or you can use rice noodles)*
6oz (175g) baby sweetcorn	
1lb (500g) courgettes	*6oz (175g) firm tofu, cut into cubes and browned in olive oil (optional)*
8oz (250g) leeks	
8oz (250g) young carrots	
2 tbs vegetable oil	*2 tbs sesame seeds*

Prepare the spring onions, ginger and garlic. Trim all the vegetables and slice them finely, diagonally.

Heat the oil in a wok and add all the prepared vegetables plus the spring onions, ginger and garlic. Stir-fry briskly together for 4–5 minutes. Add the soy sauce and black bean sauce and stir-fry for a further 2 minutes, then cover and cook gently for 5 minutes or until all the vegetables are tender but still slightly crisp.

Add the dark sesame oil. Add the cooked noodles and the browned tofu, if using, and toss to mix with the vegetables. Sprinkle with the sesame seeds, and serve immediately.

Stir-frying

A quick, easy and tasty way of cooking vegetables, this is best done in a wok, but failing that you can use a large frying pan. Cut your fresh vegetables into bite-size pieces, diagonally if you prefer; in some cases they need to be shredded or sliced finely and this can be done very quickly in the food processor.

Heat a very little oil in your wok or pan and smear it over the surface. Groundnut oil is excellent for stir-frying because it is tasteless and doesn't burn easily. Olive oil is also good, but don't use your best quality for this – leave that for salad dressings. Get the oil – and the pan – really hot before you toss in the vegetables, letting the heat sear them as you stir them in the pan. When they are evenly heated through and beginning to cook, turn the heat down a little and stir and toss constantly until they are tender but still crisp. At this point add other seasonings recommended in the recipe. In some cases you then turn the heat right down, cover with a lid and allow the vegetables to steam to a finish.

Always serve stir-fried vegetables as soon as possible after cooking as they are at their best crisp and hot from the pan.

OPPOSITE: Stir-fry of Spring Vegetables with Noodles

BEST VEGETABLE PAELLA

This great classic dish from Spain is an eye-catching meal for special occasions. The traditional fish is replaced by mushrooms, artichoke hearts, mangetout and water chestnuts. The subtle flavour of saffron permeates the dish and gives it its lovely golden colour. Serve with a watercress salad (see page 136) and fresh, warm bread.

FOR 4-6

1 oz (25g) margarine	*6 oz (175g) button mushrooms, quartered*
2 tbs vegetable oil	
1 large Spanish onion, chopped	*4 large tomatoes, skinned and chopped (fresh or canned)*
12 oz (350g) long-grain rice	
1½ pints (900ml) vegetable stock	*8 oz (250g) cooked artichoke hearts, halved*
large pinch of saffron strands, soaked in a little stock	*6 oz (175g) mangetout, steamed and sliced diagonally*
4 cloves garlic, chopped	*4 oz (125g) canned water chestnuts, drained and sliced*
6 oz (175g) frozen peas, thawed	*sea salt and freshly ground black pepper*
2 canned pimientos, chopped, or 1 large fresh red pepper, skinned and chopped	*finely grated cheese to hand around*

Heat the margarine and oil in a large pan or wok. Add the chopped onion and cook over a gentle heat for about 10 minutes or until soft and translucent. Add the rice and cook over moderate heat, stirring constantly, for a couple of minutes. Then begin to add the stock, a little at a time, and simmer until each addition is absorbed. After about 10 minutes, add the saffron and the garlic. Continue cooking for 5 minutes or so or until the rice is tender. Then stir in the rest of the ingredients and stir until heated through. Check the seasoning and serve, with grated cheese to hand around.

Skinning Peppers

Cut peppers into quarters and deseed. Cut each quarter into two or three strips and place skin-side up under a hot grill. Grill for 5–6 minutes or until the skin has blistered and blackened. Remove, place in a brown paper bag and cool. The skin will peel off easily.

Skinning Tomatoes

Put tomatoes into a large bowl and cover with boiling water. Leave to stand for about 5 minutes. Lift out one by one and pierce the skin with a sharp knife; the skin will peel off easily.

OPPOSITE: Best Vegetable Paella

NOODLE BAKE

An easy to make and unusual version of macaroni cheese, this nutritious bake contains cottage and Cheddar cheeses, milk and soured cream, and is seasoned with fresh herbs. Serve with green vegetables cooked until just tender but still crisp.

FOR 4

8oz (250g) egg noodles	*1 tbs chopped mixed fresh herbs*
½ pint (300ml) soured cream	
6oz (175g) cottage cheese	*1 tbs chopped chives*
5oz (150g) Cheddar cheese, grated finely	*sea salt and freshly ground black pepper*
4 fl oz (125ml) skimmed or soya milk	

Cook the noodles in boiling water, then drain and rinse under cold water. Mix together the soured cream, cottage cheese and 4oz (125g) of the Cheddar and stir in the milk. Add the herbs and season to taste. Mix thoroughly into the noodles.

Grease an 8 inch (20 cm) soufflé dish or other deep baking dish. Tip the noodle mixture into it and sprinkle the remaining Cheddar cheese on top. Bake at 180°C/350°F/gas 4 for 20–25 minutes. Serve hot.

Noodles

Noodles are made from a simple paste of flour (usually wheat flour) and water, sometimes some oil, and a little salt. Egg noodles have egg in the original paste and are therefore a slightly richer version of noodle.

BAKED SWEETCORN PUDDING

You can enjoy this savoury pudding hot or warm. Adding canned mild chillies is a delicious touch. The golden colour of all that sweetcorn makes a beautiful dish to look at, too!

FOR 3–4

1½oz (40g) margarine	*1 x 14oz (400g) can sweetcorn, drained*
1 medium onion, chopped finely	
1 large clove garlic, crushed	*1 x 4oz (125g) can mild chillies, drained and chopped (optional)*
1oz (25g) plain flour	
1 tsp ground mace (optional)	*½ tsp sea salt*
¼ pint (150ml) skimmed or soya milk	*freshly ground black pepper*
	3 free-range eggs, beaten

Melt the margarine in a saucepan and cook the onion and garlic over a gentle heat, covered with a lid, for 10 minutes or until quite soft, stirring from time to time. Sift the flour with the mace, if using, then stir into the softened vegetables. Gradually add the milk, stirring all the time. When smoothly blended, cook gently for 1 minute more.

Remove from the heat and stir in the sweetcorn, the optional chillies, the salt and pepper to taste. Stir in the beaten eggs.

Pour into a greased 8–9 inch (20–22.5 cm) soufflé dish or other deep baking dish. Bake at 180°C/350°F/gas 4 for 40–45 minutes or until the centre of the pudding is just set.

LANCASHIRE HOT POT WITH BUTTER BEANS ᵥ

*L*ong slow cooking brings out all the flavours of the ingredients in this hot pot to perfection, and fills the kitchen with wonderful appetizing smells.

FOR 6

1 lb (500g) vegetarian steak chunks

vegetable oil

12 oz (350g) onions, sliced

1 lb (500g) potatoes, peeled and sliced

1 x 14 oz (400g) can butter beans, drained (or equivalent cooked dried, see page 185)

1 tbs dried mixed herbs

sea salt and freshly ground black pepper

1½–2 pints (900 ml–1.2 litres) vegetable stock

Brown the steak chunks in a little oil. Layer the steak chunks, onions, potatoes and butter beans in a casserole. Season as you go with the herbs, lots of pepper and a little salt. Pour in the stock.

Cover the casserole tightly with a lid and cook at 200°C/400°F/gas 6 for 30 minutes. Turn the heat down to 170°C/325°F/gas 3 and cook for another 30 minutes. Allow to cool a little before serving, with steamed vegetables such as cauliflower, broccoli or leeks.

BELOW: Lancashire Hot Pot with Butter Beans

MEATLESS LOAF

The art of the meatless loaf is to tailor it to your taste – add your family's favourite spices or herbs, plus chopped, cooked vegetables of your choice to ring the changes. Peas, celery, leeks, broccoli and sweetcorn will all give interesting tastes and textures to the basic loaf here. Instead of the stock, you can add a 14 oz (400 g) can of chopped tomatoes with their juices, to make a very moist and tomatoey-tasting loaf.

FOR 6

1 lb (500 g) vegetarian mince	*1 tbs chopped mixed fresh thyme and sage*
1 onion, chopped and softened in a little olive oil	*1–2 tsp ground mace, or 1 tsp chilli powder or ground allspice (optional)*
4-6 oz (125-175 g) button mushrooms, sliced	
2 oz (50 g) fresh breadcrumbs	*2 tbs tomato purée*
2 free-range eggs, beaten well	*freshly ground black pepper*
¾ pint (450 ml) vegetable stock	

Mix all the ingredients together in a large bowl, or blend in a food processor. Pack into a well-greased 2 lb (1 kg) loaf tin and bake at 180°C/350°F/gas 4 for 1 hour or until crisp on top and set through. Leave to cool in the tin for at least 15 minutes before turning out. If you are cooking ahead of time, loosen the edges after 15 minutes, and turn out when cold.

Serve with rich tomato sauce (see page 151) and Yorkshire puddings (see opposite).

Dealing with Onions

Peeling pungent onions can make your eyes water, so work near the cold tap and rinse your hands frequently – it will reduce the effect of the onions.

Softening onions in oil or margarine, which is such a basic step in so many recipes, is best done by first tossing the sliced or chopped onions in the oil or fat over a moderate heat until well coated and then turning the heat down very low, covering the pan with a lid and leaving the onions to cook very gently for 10–12 minutes. They become very soft and sweet because this process steams them rather than browns them. Stir just once or twice during the cooking.

Browning onions is done over a higher heat – and they taste much stronger than onions softened by the method above.

YORKSHIRE PUDDINGS

Yorkshire puddings are very simple to make in the blender – in a matter of seconds your batter is ready. Always leave the batter to stand in a cool place, or the refrigerator, for an hour before using so that the flour can absorb the liquids fully.

MAKES 12

8oz (250g) plain flour, sifted	*1 pint (600ml) skimmed or*
¼ tsp sea salt	*soya milk*
2 free-range eggs	*vegetable oil for the tins*

Put the ingredients into the blender and blend until the batter is smooth. Leave to stand for 1 hour.

Pour a little oil into each of 12 individual deep bun tins or American muffin tins and heat in the oven at 220°C/425°F/gas 7 for 3–4 minutes. Spoon the batter into the tins and return to the oven. Bake for 10 minutes, then turn the heat down to 190°C/375°F/gas 5 and bake for a further 15 minutes or until risen and golden brown. Serve as soon as possible.

TOAD IN THE HOLE

Crisp, tasty sausages inside a cloud of light, golden batter makes irresistible and popular family food. Here is the meatless version of this classic recipe.

FOR 4–6

8oz (250g) plain flour	*6 large vegetarian sausages*
¼ tsp sea salt	*4 tbs vegetable oil, plus extra*
2 free-range eggs	*for frying the sausages*
1 pint (600ml) skimmed or	
soya milk	

Sift the flour with the salt and put into the blender with the eggs and milk. Blend to a smooth batter, and leave to stand for 1 hour.

Lightly brown the sausages in a frying pan.

Heat the 4 tbs vegetable oil in a 10 inch (25 cm) square baking pan at 220°C/425°F/gas 7 for 5 minutes. Place the sausages in the oil and pour the batter over the top. Return to the oven and bake for 15 minutes, then turn the heat down to 190°C/375°F/gas 5 and bake for a further 20 minutes or until the batter is cooked through and golden.

Serve with tomato sauce (page 151) or a salsa (page 152).

NEXT SPREAD: The main dishes for a satisfying Sunday lunch here are Meatless Loaf and Yorkshire Puddings, and Aubergine and Herb Casserole, served with Potato and Cabbage Mash (see page 106), gravy (see page 155) and carrots.

AUBERGINE AND HERB CASSEROLE

I made this recipe when I was a young girl, and recently cooked it for Pierre Franey of the New York Times on his 'Great Cooks' series. It is best eaten with a tossed salad, such as potato and cos lettuce (see page 130), and either plain pasta or fresh bread, and goes down well with a glass of red wine.

FOR 8

3½lb (1.5kg) ripe plum tomatoes, skinned (see page 59), or 2 x 1½lb (700g) cans plum tomatoes, drained

8 tbs olive oil

1 large onion, chopped

2 tbs chopped garlic

6oz (175g) tomato purée

1 tbs each chopped fresh oregano, basil and thyme

2lb (1kg) aubergines, sliced diagonally ¼ inch (0.5cm) thick

plain flour

sea salt and freshly ground black pepper

8oz (250g) mozzarella cheese, sliced

Chop the fresh or canned tomatoes into small cubes. Heat 1 tbs of the olive oil in a saucepan and sauté the onion and garlic, stirring, for 1 minute. Add the chopped tomatoes and the tomato purée, and then the herbs. Stir well and bring to a simmer. Cover and cook over a very low heat for 30 minutes.

Meanwhile, dredge the slices of aubergine in flour and sauté them in the rest of the olive oil in a large pan over moderate heat until lightly browned on both sides.

Season the tomato sauce. Pour a layer of tomato sauce over the bottom of a baking dish and cover with a layer of aubergine slices. Continue making layers, finishing with a layer of aubergines. Arrange the sliced mozzarella over the top. Bake at 180°C/350°F/gas 4 for 1 hour or until golden brown.

COTTAGE CRUNCH CASSEROLE

This layered casserole is special enough to be the main dish for Christmas dinner, or for other holiday or special occasion menus. Serve with the cheese and parsley sauce on page 155 and lots of roasted vegetables. Cranberry sauce will be welcome too.

FOR 8

1 lb (500g) vegetarian mince

2 free-range eggs, beaten well

¾ pint (450 ml) water

8 oz (250g) leeks, chopped and cooked in boiling water for 10 minutes

6 oz (175g) mushrooms, sliced

2 oz (50g) walnut pieces, chopped

1 tsp each ground mace and allspice, or 1-2 tsp curry powder (optional)

few drops of Tabasco sauce (optional)

12 oz (350g) courgettes, steamed and sliced

6 oz (175g) mangetout, steamed

4 sun-dried tomatoes in oil, chopped finely

3 tbs chopped mixed fresh herbs, e.g. parsley, fennel, coriander, marjoram, tarragon

4 oz (125g) mozzarella cheese, sliced

3 oz (75g) Cheddar cheese, grated

Mix the mince with the beaten eggs and stir in the water. Allow to soak for 30 minutes, then purée in the blender until fairly smooth. Add the prepared leeks, mushrooms and walnuts and season with the optional spices and Tabasco. Don't add salt as the vegetarian mince is sufficiently salty.

Grease a large baking dish. Spread half of the mince mixture on the bottom. Layer the sliced courgettes, mangetout, tomatoes, herbs and mozzarella over the top, and cover with the rest of the mince mixture. Sprinkle the grated cheese over the top. Bake at 180°C/350°F/gas 4 for 1 hour.

Fresh and Home-dried Herbs

When herbs are in season – from late spring through summer – they can be used to impart wonderful flavours and fragrances to food. Fresh herbs make a distinct difference to cooked dishes, and they are delicious in salads. When fresh herbs are out of season or unavailable, dried herbs are an excellent substitute for fresh in soups, casseroles and meatless dishes.

If you grow your own herbs you can dry them quite successfully yourself. Pick them in the morning when they are at the height of their fragrance. You can then either lay them on paper in a warm place to dry out, or tie them into small bunches and hang them in a warm, dry place with plenty of air circulating around them. When brittle – after several days – strip them off their stalks and store in dark jars out of direct sunlight.

STUFFED PEPPERS ᵥ

This dish is inspired by the cookery of the Middle East, where stuffed vegetables of all kinds play an important part. You can make the stuffing with vegetarian mince or without, adding another 2 oz (50 g) rice in its place if you prefer.

MAKES 6

3 peppers	3 tbs chopped parsley
1 large onion, chopped finely	1 tsp each ground cumin and
2 tbs olive oil	allspice or to taste (optional)
1 clove garlic, crushed	½ tsp chilli powder (optional)
(optional)	4 oz (125 g) vegetarian mince
8 oz (250 g) tomatoes, skinned	3 oz (75 g) long-grain rice,
(see page 59) and chopped	cooked (see page 96)
3 sun-dried tomatoes in oil,	2 oz (50 g) pine nuts
chopped (optional)	

Halve each pepper and scoop out the seeds.

Soften the onion in the oil for 7–8 minutes over a low heat, covered with a lid. If using the garlic, add for the last 2–3 minutes of cooking. When soft, add the tomatoes, the optional sun-dried tomatoes and the parsley and stir well. Then add the optional spices and cook gently for a minute longer. Stir in the rest of the ingredients.

Pack the mixture into the pepper halves. Place in a greased baking dish. Pour in hot water to cover the bottom of the dish, cover with foil and bake at 190°C/375°F/gas 5 for 30 minutes. Remove the foil and bake for a further 15 minutes.

QUICK MEATLESS STROGANOFF

This is sensational: a great classic recipe adapted for people who prefer to eat a meatless diet. It is lovely with noodles or rice. An amazing dish with wonderful flavours – lighter and even more epicurean than the original!

FOR 4–6

2 oz (50 g) margarine	2 tbs olive oil
2 onions, sliced	8 oz (250 g) vegetarian steak
2 tbs plain flour	chunks
¼ pint (150 ml) vegetable stock	½ pint (300 ml) soured cream
½ pint (300 ml) white wine	freshly ground black pepper
8 oz (250 g) small mushrooms,	chopped parsley to garnish
cut in half	

Heat the margarine in a saucepan and cook the onions, covered, until soft. Add the flour and stir it in well, then stir in the stock followed by the white wine. Add the mushrooms. Simmer gently, uncovered, for about 5 minutes, stirring occasionally.

Meanwhile, heat the oil and toss the steak chunks until browned all over. Mix them into the mushroom sauce. Stir in the soured cream, season with lots of pepper and cook very gently (without boiling) for 6–8 minutes. Serve sprinkled with chopped parsley.

OPPOSITE: Stuffed Peppers

MUSHROOM MOUSSAKA

A great dish for a supper party. Serve with your favourite rice dish and a seasonal salad such as the rocket and spinach salad on page 129. Add a basket of crusty bread and a bottle of retsina – and transport yourselves to the Mediterranean!

FOR 6

2 medium aubergines, sliced

5 tbs olive oil

sea salt and freshly ground black pepper

1 large onion, sliced

1 clove garlic, crushed

1½ lb (750g) flat mushrooms, or wild mushrooms if available, sliced

1 x 14 oz (400g) can tomatoes, drained and chopped, or 6 large fresh tomatoes, skinned (see page 59) and chopped

1 tbs balsamic vinegar or fresh lemon juice

4 tbs chopped parsley

1 tbs each chopped fresh marjoram and thyme

1¼ lb (625g) potatoes, peeled and boiled 'al dente', then sliced

8 oz (250g) vegetarian mince browned in 1 tbs vegetable oil (optional)

2 oz (50g) ricotta cheese

¾ pint (450ml) béchamel sauce (see page 155)

2 tbs grated Cheddar cheese

Brush the aubergine slices with 3 tbs of the olive oil and sprinkle them with salt. Arrange in a single layer on a baking tray and bake at 180°C/350°F/gas 4 for 15 minutes.

In a large pan heat the rest of the olive oil and soften the onion and garlic, covered, for 10 minutes over a medium to low heat. Stir occasionally. Then add the mushrooms and toss thoroughly. Cook, partially covered with a lid, until they have softened. Add the chopped tomatoes, vinegar or lemon juice, parsley, marjoram and thyme and mix well. Season to taste with sea salt and freshly ground black pepper. Simmer for 5 minutes.

Make a layer of the potato slices in the bottom of a shallow baking dish. Continue making layers with the aubergines, mushroom mixture, remaining potatoes and optional vegetarian mince. Finish with aubergines. Press down. Stir the ricotta into the béchamel until well blended and spoon evenly over the surface. Sprinkle with the grated cheese. Bake at 180°C/350°F/gas 4 for 40–45 minutes.

Wild Mushrooms

There is a wonderful choice of wild mushrooms if you wish to harvest your own from the woods and fields. Chanterelles, puffballs, morels, boletus and field mushrooms all have unique flavours which are superb in a variety of recipes. Always take a good field guide with you, however, to make sure you have picked the right mushroom. A few wild mushrooms are poisonous.

Failing the mushroom-hike, try the Chinese mushrooms commonly sold in supermarkets – shiitake and oyster mushrooms have their own distinctive and delicate flavour.

CRISPY MUSHROOM LAYERS v

ayers of a crisp crumb and nut mixture surround a garlicky mushroom filling. Delicious! Serve with baked potatoes and the special rocket salad on page 129.

FOR 4–6

6 oz (175g) wholemeal breadcrumbs	*1 x 14 oz (400g) can tomatoes, drained and chopped, or 6 large fresh tomatoes, skinned (see page 59) and chopped*
4 oz (125g) mixed nuts, finely chopped	
3 oz (75g) margarine	*2 cloves garlic, crushed*
1 large onion, chopped finely	*2 tsp dried mixed herbs*
10 oz (300g) flat mushrooms, sliced	*sea salt and freshly ground black pepper*

Mix the crumbs and nuts together. Melt 2 oz (50 g) of the margarine and fry this mixture until golden. Set aside.

Melt the rest of the margarine in another pan, add the onion, cover and cook over a low heat for 5–8 minutes or until softened. Add the sliced mushrooms and toss thoroughly, then cover the pan again and cook gently for 3–4 minutes. Add the tomatoes, garlic and herbs and stir well. Season to taste.

Make a layer of half of the breadcrumb mixture on the bottom of a baking dish and place the mushroom filling on top. Finish with a layer of the remaining crumb mixture. Bake at 190°C/375°F/ gas 5 for 30 minutes or until crisp and golden. Serve piping hot.

MEATLESS MEATBALLS WITH SAUCES

These are crisp on the outside and fine and smooth inside, and are quite delicious with a variety of different sauces such as roasted red pepper sauce (see page 149), the chilli sauce on page 152, the tarragon and mustard sauce on page 149 or the sauce of mixed wild mushrooms (page 154). Serve with a potato dish of your choice. You can also shape the mixture into vegetarian burgers.

MAKES 12

8oz (250g) vegetarian mince	*2 free-range eggs, beaten*
1 onion, chopped finely	*sea salt and freshly ground*
1oz (25g) Cheddar cheese,	*black pepper*
grated	*ground mace and allspice*
2 tbs chopped fresh mixed	*(optional)*
herbs, or 1½ tsp dried mixed	*plain flour*
herbs	*vegetable oil*
1oz (25g) fresh breadcrumbs	

Mix the vegetarian mince with the onion, cheese, herbs, breadcrumbs and eggs in the blender. Blend until the mixture is smooth and quite fine. Season to taste with salt and pepper and add a little optional spice to taste. At this point you can also add grated courgette, shredded leek or some cooked spinach, if you like.

Form into small meatballs and roll in flour to coat lightly. Fry in hot shallow vegetable oil over moderate heat until nicely browned all over. Drain on kitchen paper and serve hot.

OPPOSITE: Meatless Meatballs with Chilli Sauce and Tarragon and Mustard Sauce

SIMPLE VEGETABLE CURRY ❧

You can vary the vegetables endlessly for this 'dry' curry, according to season and your choice – leeks, cauliflower and broccoli are all delicious spiced, as are French beans, mangetout or sweetcorn. You can also add browned vegetarian steak chunks and let them heat through in the sauce for the last 10 minutes of cooking.

FOR 3–4

1 large onion, sliced	*1 large potato, scrubbed and diced*
2 cloves garlic, sliced	
2 tbs olive oil	*8oz (250g) carrots, sliced*
2 tbs Madras curry paste or to taste	*8oz (250g) courgettes, diced*
	4oz (125g) mushrooms, sliced
6oz (175g) frozen peas, thawed	

Soften the onion and garlic gently in the oil over a low heat, covered with a lid, for 10 minutes. Stir occasionally. When they are soft add the curry paste and stir for a few moments, then add the prepared vegetables. Toss until they are all well coated with the curried onion mixture. Cover tightly with a lid and cook over a very low heat for 30–40 minutes or until the vegetables are tender. (This steams the vegetables, bringing out all their flavours, and their juices run so you don't need to add stock.)

When they are cooked, remove from the heat and allow to stand until you are ready to eat – this dish improves on resting. Serve with plain or fried rice, and naan bread.

EASY CAULIFLOWER DHAL ❧

A lovely 'dry' dhal with gentle spicing, this Indian dish goes beautifully with Chinese egg fried rice (see page 94), some cucumber raita and a crisp green salad.

FOR 4–6

8oz (250g) green lentils, soaked for 1-2 hours	*3 cloves garlic, chopped finely*
	2 tbs olive oil
1 large onion, sliced	*2 tsp each ground turmeric, coriander and cumin or to taste*
2 inches (5cm) root ginger, bruised	
1 tbs chopped parsley	*1 cauliflower, cut into florets and cooked*
1 fresh green chilli	
	sea salt

Drain the lentils and put them into a saucepan with the onion, piece of ginger, parsley and whole chilli. Cover with water, bring to the boil and simmer for 30 minutes.

Meanwhile, cook the garlic gently in the oil for 3–4 minutes or until soft, then stir in the ground spices. Toss the cauliflower florets in the spiced mixture until well coated, and season to taste with sea salt.

Drain the lentils, remove the ginger and chilli and mix thoroughly with the spiced cauliflower.

CURRIED CHICK PEAS WITH ONIONS ▾

A deliciously spicy dish which is simple to prepare, and very nutritious. Serve spooned over plain boiled rice or the saffron rice on page 94, with pitta bread or naan.

FOR 4

2 tbs olive oil	*2 x 14oz (400g) cans chick*
2 onions, thinly sliced	*peas*
2 cloves garlic, crushed	*3 tbs fresh lemon juice*
2 tbs sesame seeds	*1 tsp tamari or light soy sauce*
1 tbs curry powder or to taste	*3 tbs chopped fresh parsley*
sea salt	*freshly cooked rice to serve*

Heat the oil in a large frying pan and cook the onion and garlic very gently, covered, for about 25 minutes or until meltingly soft and golden. Stir in the sesame seeds and curry powder. Season with salt. Cook uncovered for 5 minutes, stirring occasionally.

Drain the chick peas, reserving 4 fl oz (125 ml) of the liquid. Add the chick peas to the pan with the reserved liquid and cook, stirring frequently, until the chick peas are hot and almost all the liquid has evaporated.

Stir in the lemon juice, tamari and parsley. Serve hot, spooned over rice.

BELOW: Curried Chick Peas with Onions

SUMMER STEW WITH VEGETABLES ᵥ

A satisfying stew for people who don't want to eat meat but still like its texture. You can, of course, vary the vegetables – for a more exotic combination try okra, broccoli, runner or French beans, aubergines and peppers. You can alter the spicing too, to your taste, adding mace or chilli for example.

FOR 4

1 large onion, sliced

1 large clove garlic, sliced

2 tbs olive oil

1 baby turnip, cubed

6oz (175g) young carrots, sliced

6oz (175g) new potatoes, washed and diced

6oz (175g) cauliflower florets

8oz (250g) baby courgettes, sliced

1 pint (600ml) vegetable stock

2 heaped tbs cornflour, mixed with 3 tbs water

1 x 14oz (400g) can chopped tomatoes with juice

3-4 tbs chopped fresh parsley, thyme, tarragon or other mixed herbs

optional spices, to taste

sea salt and freshly ground pepper

3 tbs vegetable oil

8oz (250g) vegetarian steak chunks

In a large pan, soften the onion and garlic in the olive oil, covered, over a low heat. Then add the prepared vegetables and brown for 5–6 minutes, stirring and turning. Gradually add the stock, stirring, and bring to the boil, then stir in the cornflour and water mixture. Add the tomatoes with their juice and stir well. Add the herbs, plus any spices that you choose. Season to taste. Turn the heat right down and cover the pan tightly. Simmer gently for 25 minutes, stirring occasionally.

Meanwhile heat the vegetable oil in a shallow pan and brown the steak chunks all over for about 3 minutes. Stir the steak chunks into the stew, cover again and cook gently for a further 10 minutes. Check the seasoning, and it is ready to serve.

OPPOSITE: Summer Stew with Vegetables

SPINACH PANCAKES WITH MUSHROOMS

*A*lthough this takes a little time to prepare, it is well worth the work! The spinach pancakes are wrapped around a garlicky mushroom filling, and finished off in the oven with a topping of melting mozzarella. A lovely supper dish, served with a sauce of your choice plus steamed vegetables and a fennel salad (see page 134) or green bean salad (page 141).

FOR 4 (Makes 8)

4oz (125g) plain flour	*1oz (25g) margarine*
sea salt and freshly ground black pepper	*1¼ lb (625g) mushrooms, sliced thinly*
1 free-range egg, beaten	*3 large cloves garlic, crushed*
½ pint (300ml) skimmed or soya milk	*1oz (25g) plain flour*
6oz (175g) cooked spinach (from 14oz/400g fresh), thoroughly drained (squeeze in your hands to remove excess water)	*3 fl oz (75ml) skimmed or soya milk*
	grated nutmeg
	4oz (125g) mozzarella cheese, diced
vegetable oil	*parsley to garnish*

Sift the flour and seasonings into the blender, add the egg and milk and blend until smooth. Add the spinach and blend again. Thin out the batter if necessary with more milk – the consistency depends on the amount of water in the spinach.

Brush an 8 inch (20 cm) frying pan with oil, heat it, then add 2 ladles-full of the pancake batter. Spread it to cover the bottom of the pan evenly. Cook the pancake for 1 minute before turning to brown the other side. Keep it warm while you cook the remaining pancakes.

Heat the margarine in another pan and cook the mushrooms with the garlic for 3–4 minutes or until the juices run. Stir in the flour to soak them up, then gradually add the milk a little at a time, stirring so that the sauce is smooth. Season to taste with salt, pepper and nutmeg.

Fill the pancakes with the mushroom mixture, roll them up and place in a baking dish. Scatter the mozzarella over the top and bake at 180°C/350°F/gas 4 for 15 minutes. Serve hot garnished with parsley.

OPPOSITE: Spinach Pancakes with Mushrooms, served with Green Bean Salad

LAYERED VEGETABLE TERRINE

*F*estival and party food par excellence, this beautiful three-coloured loaf makes a meal for special occasions. It takes a while to make, but repays you handsomely.

FOR 6

1¼ lb (625g) cauliflower, steamed until tender

1¼ lb (625g) carrots, steamed until tender

12oz (350g) spinach, cooked and thoroughly drained

6 tbs crème fraîche or single cream

2 tbs chopped fresh coriander

3 spring onions, chopped finely

2 tsp ground ginger or to taste

1 tsp grated nutmeg or to taste

sea salt and freshly ground black pepper

6 free-range eggs

6oz (175g) large mushrooms, sliced

In three separate operations, purée the cauliflower, carrots and spinach, adding 2 tbs crème fraîche or single cream to each. Season the cauliflower with the chopped coriander, the carrots with the spring onions and ginger, and the spinach with the nutmeg. Add salt and freshly ground black pepper to all three mixtures. Stir 2 beaten eggs into each mixture.

Grease a 2lb (1kg) loaf tin. Place the cauliflower mixture on the bottom and arrange a layer of half the sliced mushrooms on top. Cover with the carrot mixture and add a layer of the remaining mushrooms. Finally, pour the spinach mixture over the top. Place the tin in a baking tray of hot water and bake at 200°C/400°F/gas 6 for 50–60 minutes or until a sharp knife inserted into the centre comes out clean.

Allow to stand for at least 10–15 minutes before attempting to turn out. Run a knife around the edge of the terrine to loosen the sides, then invert on to a large plate and tap the base of the tin until the terrine comes out. Serve with a wonderful sauce of your choice (see pages 149–52).

OPPOSITE: Layered Vegetable Terrine, with Roasted Red Pepper Sauce (see page 149)

VEGETABLE SOUFFLÉ

Cauliflower makes a particularly good soufflé, and there are of course endless variations on the theme. You can substitute other cooked vegetables such as spinach (6 oz/175 g) or 8 oz (250 g) of courgettes, broccoli, asparagus, mushrooms or petits pois, using this master recipe. Grated Cheddar cheese (3 oz/75 g) is another option.

FOR 4

1 tbs chopped spring onion or shallot	½ pint (300ml) hot skimmed or soya milk
½ oz (15g) margarine	pinch each of cayenne pepper and grated nutmeg
8oz (250g) cooked cauliflower florets, cut small	sea salt and freshly ground pepper
	4 free-range eggs, separated
For the soufflé base:	
2oz (50g) margarine	
1½ oz (40g) plain flour	

Soften the spring onion or shallot in the margarine, then toss in the cauliflower florets and cook gently for 2 minutes. Set aside.

To make the soufflé base, melt the margarine in a heavy saucepan and stir in the flour until smooth. Gradually add the hot milk and stir until smooth and thick. Season to taste with the spices, salt and pepper. Simmer very gently for 3–4 minutes. Off the heat, stir in the egg yolks, mixing well. Fold in the cauliflower mixture. Whisk the egg whites until very stiff, and fold carefully into the cauliflower mixture.

Spoon into a well-greased 8–9 inch (20–22.5 cm) soufflé dish and put into a 200°C/400°F/gas 6 oven. Turn the heat down to 190°C/375°F/gas 5 and bake for 25–30 minutes or until the soufflé is well risen and golden on top, but still a little creamy in the centre. Serve immediately.

GOAT'S CHEESE AND DILL SOUFFLÉ

Soufflés are very quick and easy to make once you master the basics, and there are infinite variations you can try. Lovely with new potatoes and steamed courgettes.

FOR 4

2oz (50g) margarine	2 tbs chopped fresh dill
2oz (50g) plain flour	4 free-range eggs, separated
½ pint (300ml) hot skimmed or soya milk	sea salt and freshly ground black pepper
4oz (125g) soft goat's cheese or feta cheese, cut into small cubes	

Melt the margarine in a small heavy saucepan and stir in the flour until smooth. Gradually add the hot milk and stir until smooth and thick. Simmer very gently for 3–4 minutes, then stir in the cheese and the dill. Off the heat, stir in the egg yolks and season with salt and pepper.

Whisk the egg whites until very stiff, and fold carefully into the cheese mixture. Spoon into a well buttered 8 inch (20 cm) soufflé dish and bake at 200°C/400°F/gas 6 for 20–25 minutes or until well risen and golden on top, but still creamy in the middle. Serve immediately.

82

OMELETTES

*A*n omelette is one of the simplest and quickest dishes ever. Leave it plain and serve with vegetables or a salad, or add a filling. Use fillings such as mushrooms sautéed with garlic and parsley, grated cheese, masses of chopped fresh herbs with croutons if you like, sliced tomatoes sautéed in olive oil, boiled sliced new potatoes with chives – and so on. Improvise, using your favourite vegetables and herbs!

FOR 1

2 free-range eggs	*½ oz (15g) margarine, or 2 tbs*
sea salt and freshly ground	*olive oil*
black pepper	

Beat the eggs until frothy, and season to taste. Melt the margarine, or heat the oil, in an 8 inch (20 cm) frying pan over moderate heat. When extremely hot but not smoking, pour in the eggs and let them cook, moving the mixture around a little to start with. When the upper surface begins to bubble, lift the cooked edges and allow the uncooked egg to run underneath. When the base of the omelette is lightly browned, fold in half. Cook a little longer so that the middle sets, and then flip on to a warm plate to serve.

VARIATIONS

• Separate the eggs. Whisk the whites until stiff and fold into the yolks before cooking in the hot margarine or oil.

• Instead of folding the omelette, flip it over to cook both sides evenly.

• For a filled omelette, put the filling into the centre while the base of the omelette is browning, then fold it and cook a minute longer.

FILLINGS FROM AROUND THE WORLD

SPANISH OMELETTE

Sauté finely chopped onion and celery gently in olive oil until soft. Then stir in chopped canned or fresh tomatoes and season to taste.

MEXICAN OMELETTE

Soften stoned olives, chillies and tomatoes in a little oil and season with a pinch of ground cumin.

FRENCH FINES HERBES OMELETTE

This famous recipe uses fresh garden herbs such as chives, parsley, marjoram, tarragon, fennel, basil etc, all finely chopped and tossed in a little melted butter. Add to the egg mixture before cooking.

CHINESE OMELETTE

Steam beansprouts and matchstick carrots with grated fresh ginger and add crushed garlic, sliced spring onion and a little soy sauce. You can also add some chopped fresh coriander to the egg mixture before cooking it. This omelette is traditionally served rolled rather than folded. Try cooking it in dark sesame oil for extra flavour.

CHAPTER FOUR

Pasta, Rice and Potatoes

Pasta, rice and potatoes are major cornerstones of the meatless diet, providing carbohydrate balance to the vegetable ingredients as well as satisfying bulk. They are endlessly versatile, and can be used to make main meals as well as side dishes. They are cheap, too, and always available.

At one time these starch foods were thought of as 'fattening', and were eaten sparingly or even avoided altogether by those trying to slim. But in fact, they are not fattening – it all depends what you put on them or mix them with! Cooked thoughtfully, using light sauces, mixing them with other vegetables, and flavouring them with garlic, herbs or spices, they are an important staple of a meatless diet.

SUMMER LASAGNE

*G*ood any time of year, but especially good made when the tomato crop is at its height, and courgettes and basil are at their best. The cheese melts between layers of vegetables and pasta and is mouthwatering. Great served with a seasonal salad and fresh bread.

FOR 6

2 lb (1 kg) small courgettes, steamed lightly and sliced	*3 free-range egg yolks*
sea salt and freshly ground black pepper	*For the light tomato sauce:*
	2 tbs olive oil
large bunch of fresh basil, chopped	*1 small onion, chopped finely*
	2 tsp plain flour
8 oz (250 g) cottage, ricotta, feta or soft goat's cheese, sliced if necessary	*2 lb (1 kg) ripe tomatoes, skinned (see page 59) and chopped, or equivalent canned chopped tomatoes*
8 oz (250 g) no-cook lasagne	
½ pint (300 ml) béchamel sauce (see page 155)	*small bunch of fresh herbs, chopped finely*
¼ pint (150 ml) crème fraîche or single cream	*1 inch (2.5 cm) strip of orange rind (optional)*
2 oz (50 g) cheese, grated	*sea salt to taste*

First make the tomato sauce. Heat the oil in a saucepan, add the onion and cook over a low heat, covered, for 8–10 minutes or until softened. Stir in the flour and cook gently, uncovered, for 3 minutes. Stir in the rest of the sauce ingredients. Cover the pan again and simmer for 5 minutes, then remove the lid and simmer for a further 20 minutes, stirring occasionally. Add a little water as necessary to prevent the sauce from sticking (the finished consistency should be quite thick). Discard the orange rind.

Moisten the bottom of an ovenproof dish with a little tomato sauce. Make a layer of sliced courgettes and season with salt and pepper. Sprinkle some chopped basil over them. Cover with slices of cheese and moisten with a little more tomato sauce. Cover with strips of lasagne. Continue making these layers until all the ingredients are used up, ending with a layer of lasagne.

Heat the béchamel gently and stir in the crème fraîche or single cream. Mix in the grated cheese until it melts, and season to taste. Off the heat, beat in the free-range egg yolks. Pour the sauce over the top lasagne layer and bake at 190°C/375°F/gas 5 for 1–1¼ hours or until the topping is deep golden and set.

SPAGHETTI WITH OLIVE OIL AND GARLIC

This is one of my favourites – it's so easy. I use lots of garlic, which I love, and which is very good for you. Serve with a Caesar salad (see page 133) or the watercress salad on page 136 and some fresh bread.

FOR 2

2-3 large cloves garlic (or more according to taste), crushed	*freshly grated Parmesan, to taste (optional)*
3 tbs olive oil	*chopped fresh herbs such as parsley, basil and oregano, to taste*
freshly ground black pepper	
6oz (175g) spaghetti	

Stir the crushed garlic into the olive oil and add masses of freshly ground black pepper.

Cook the spaghetti until 'al dente' (see page 90) and drain well. Mix the garlicky oil into the hot spaghetti, add Parmesan and herbs, and toss thoroughly. Serve immediately.

Vegetarian Parmesan

Parmesan cheese is traditionally made using animal rennet, and is not suitable for vegetarians. However, there are now a few brands of Parmesan on the market made with vegetable agents. If you cannot find one, substitute finely grated vegetarian Cheddar cheese.

PASTA SHELLS WITH LEEKS AND COURGETTES

Tasty and looks great too. You can substitute your favourite pasta shapes for the shells. Serve a fresh tomato salad with some mixed salad leaves alongside.

FOR 4

2-3 tbs olive oil	*2 tbs chopped fresh basil*
3 leeks, sliced finely	*sea salt and freshly ground black pepper*
4 medium courgettes, sliced finely	*cayenne pepper*
12oz (350g) pasta shells	*2oz (50g) sun-dried tomatoes in oil, sliced thinly*
4oz (125g) soft goat's cheese or feta cheese, crumbled, or Cheddar cheese, grated	*grated cheese to hand around*

Heat the olive oil in a frying pan and toss in the leeks and courgettes to coat them. Turn the heat down, cover and cook over a low heat for 10–15 minutes or until very soft. Stir occasionally. At the same time, cook the pasta until 'al dente' (see page 90).

Stir the crumbled goat's cheese into the leeks and courgettes and cook until well amalgamated. Add the basil and season to taste with salt, pepper and cayenne. Toss into the hot, well-drained pasta and sprinkle the sun-dried tomatoes over the top. Serve immediately, with grated cheese to hand around.

OPPOSITE: Spaghetti with Olive Oil and Garlic

TAGLIATELLE WITH MUSHROOM SAUCE

The lovely flavour of tarragon goes well with the gentle creamy taste of mushrooms. This is food fit for special occasions, whether formal or informal. Serve with the green bean salad on page 141 or a tossed leaf salad and some bread on the side.

FOR 4

1 large onion, chopped	squeeze of lemon juice
2 cloves garlic, sliced finely	sea salt and freshly ground black pepper
2 tbs olive oil	
1 lb (500g) mushrooms	freshly grated nutmeg (optional)
2 tbs each chopped fresh parsley and tarragon	grated cheese to hand around
1 lb (500g) tagliatelle	
7 fl oz (200ml) crème fraîche or single cream	

Cook the chopped onion and garlic in the oil, covered, over a gentle heat for 8–10 minutes or until softened. Put the mushrooms in the blender or food processor and run it until they are very finely chopped (or else chop them very finely indeed by hand). Add them to the pan with the herbs and cook for a further 6–8 minutes. At the same time, cook the pasta until 'al dente' (see page 90).

Stir the crème fraîche or single cream into the sauce and heat through gently. Add the lemon juice and season to taste with salt, pepper and nutmeg.

Mix this sauce into the hot, well-drained tagliatelle and serve immediately, with grated cheese to hand around.

PASTA TWISTS WITH SPINACH AND NUTS

Crème fraîche is soured pasteurized cream. It is lighter than double cream and gives a delicious taste to pasta sauces. It combines beautifully with the strong flavour of spinach and the crunchy texture of the nuts.

FOR 4

1 tbs olive oil	12 oz (350g) pasta twists
3 spring onions, chopped	¼ pint (150ml) crème fraîche or single cream
1-2 cloves garlic, crushed	
8 oz (250g) fresh young spinach, chopped finely	2 oz (50g) walnut pieces or pecans, chopped
1 tbs chopped fresh tarragon or 1 tsp dried tarragon (optional)	sea salt and freshly ground black pepper
	grated cheese to hand around

Heat the olive oil in a frying pan or wok and soften the spring onions and garlic for 1–2 minutes. Add the chopped spinach and optional tarragon and stir-fry for 3–4 minutes. At the same time cook the pasta until 'al dente' (see page 90). Stir the crème fraîche and walnuts into the spinach mixture and season to taste. Heat through.

Pour the sauce over the hot, well drained pasta and toss gently. Serve with grated cheese to hand around.

SPINACH FETTUCCINE WITH CREAMY TOMATOES AND BASIL

*T*his is a pasta dish you can run up in next to no time. Serve with French or Italian bread and a tossed green salad or the roasted pepper salad on page 139.

FOR 3–4

1 x 14oz (400g) can chopped tomatoes with their juice, or 12oz (350g) fresh tomatoes, skinned (see page 59) and chopped

2 tbs olive oil

3 cloves garlic, sliced finely

large bunch of fresh basil, chopped roughly

sea salt and freshly ground black pepper

½ pint (300ml) crème fraîche or single cream

8oz (250g) spinach fettuccine

2oz (50g) Cheddar cheese, finely grated

Mix the tomatoes with the olive oil, garlic and basil, and season to taste with salt and pepper. Heat very gently so the flavours blend together, then add the crème fraîche or single cream and stir until smoothly blended. Leave to warm over the lowest possible heat.

Cook the spinach fettuccine until 'al dente' (see page 90) and drain thoroughly. Toss with the sauce. Add the grated Cheddar and toss again. Serve with more grated cheese to hand around.

PENNE WITH TOMATOES AND MOZZARELLA

*T*his fresh tomato sauce takes only minutes to prepare and is best made with full-flavoured vine-ripened tomatoes in season. The dish goes beautifully with a crisp green salad or the shredded courgette salad on page 141.

FOR 4

2 tbs olive oil

3 tbs fresh basil, torn into small pieces

6 fresh tomatoes, cut into small squares

6oz (175g) mozzarella cheese, cut into small squares

8 sun-dried tomatoes in oil, chopped (optional)

sea salt and freshly ground black pepper

12oz (350g) penne

Put the oil, basil, tomatoes, mozzarella and optional sun-dried tomatoes into a bowl. Season to taste with salt and lots of freshly ground pepper. Leave to stand while you prepare the pasta.

Cook the penne until it is 'al dente' (see page 90) and drain well. Toss the hot pasta in the sauce and serve at once.

SPAGHETTINI WITH SUN-DRIED TOMATOES, AUBERGINES AND CHILLI

*U*sing fine spaghetti adds finesse to this recipe, but if you want to vary your pasta meals you can use Japanese buckwheat noodles for this dish. Like spaghettini they are very fine, but flat, and their flavour is gorgeous. The bite of chilli in the sauce is an inspired contrast to the softness of the aubergine.

FOR 4

4 shallots, sliced finely

2 cloves garlic, sliced finely

2 tbs olive oil

1 medium aubergine, cut into small cubes

1 tsp dried mixed herbs

3 oz (75g) sun-dried tomatoes in oil, sliced

1-2 fresh chillies (according to taste), deseeded and sliced very finely, or 1 x 4oz (125g) can mild chillies, drained and chopped finely

7 fl oz (200ml) crème fraîche or single cream

12 oz (350g) spaghettini

sea salt

grated cheese to hand around

Cook the shallots and garlic in the oil, covered, for 5–6 minutes or until soft. Stir in the aubergine and cook for 2–3 minutes. Add the herbs, sun-dried tomatoes and chillies and stir well to mix. Turn the heat down to very low, cover again and steam for 10 minutes, stirring occasionally. Then add the crème fraîche or single cream and heat through for a further 5 minutes. At the same time, cook the spaghettini until 'al dente' (see below).

Purée the aubergine mixture in a blender or food processor, or mash to a paste, and season to taste with salt.

Toss the sauce into the hot, well-drained spaghettini and serve immediately, with grated cheese to hand around.

How to Cook Pasta

1. Bring water (3½ pints/2 litres per 8oz/250g pasta) to the boil with 1 tsp olive oil in a large pan and add a generous pinch of sea salt.

2. Put the pasta into the water and bring back to the boil. Simmer over a moderate heat for the shortest cooking time recommended on the packet. Stir from time to time. Alternatively, put the pasta into the boiling water and bring back to the boil, then remove the pan from the heat and cover with a lid. Leave to stand off the heat for the cooking time recommended on the packet, stirring from time to time.

3. To test the pasta, lift out a piece on a long-handled fork or slotted spoon: it is done when it is tender but still firm to the bite ('al dente'). Never overcook pasta.

4. Drain it in a colander, shaking well to remove all excess water. Serve immediately.

OPPOSITE: Spaghettini with Sun-dried Tomatoes, Aubergines and Chilli

WINTER LASAGNE

One of the joys of this dish is that it is so easy to prepare, especially when you use the lasagne that requires no pre-cooking. It can also be made well in advance and popped into the oven when you are ready to cook it. All it needs is a Caesar salad (see page 133) and warm granary bread.

FOR 6

12 oz (350 g) mushrooms, sliced	*crushed garlic to taste*
5 tbs vegetable oil	*dried mixed herbs*
12 oz (350 g) vegetarian mince	*8 oz (250 g) no-cook lasagne*
1 onion, chopped finely	*1 lb (500 g) fresh spinach, cooked and drained well then chopped*
1 x 1½ lb (700 g) can tomatoes, drained and roughly chopped, or 1¼ lb (625 g) fresh tomatoes, skinned (see page 59) and chopped	*¾ pint (450 ml) béchamel sauce (see page 155)*
sea salt and freshly ground black pepper	*3 oz (75 g) cheese, grated*
	2 free-range eggs, beaten

Sauté the mushrooms briskly in 3 tbs of hot oil until they are lightly cooked and crisp. Set aside. Mix the vegetarian mince with the chopped onion and cook in the rest of the oil for 4–5 minutes or until the onion softens a little.

Cover the bottom of an ovenproof dish with chopped tomatoes and season with salt and pepper, some crushed garlic and a sprinkling of dried mixed herbs. Cover with lasagne strips and make the next layer with the mince mixture. Season again. Spread spinach on top and then mushrooms. Continue making layers, finishing with a layer of lasagne.

Heat the béchamel gently and stir in the grated cheese until it melts. Remove from the heat and stir in the beaten free-range eggs. Pour over the top of the lasagne, and bake at 190°C/375°F/gas 5 for 1 hour or until well browned on top.

SPINACH FUSILLI BAKE

The original combination of layers – spinach, garlicky pasta and sliced tomatoes topped with cheese – makes a memorable meal served with Caesar salad (see page 133) and fresh granary bread.

FOR 3–4

1 lb (500 g) spinach, steamed	*10 oz (300 g) fusilli, cooked until 'al dente' (see page 90)*
¾ pint (450 ml) béchamel sauce (see page 155)	*2 tbs olive oil*
sea salt and freshly ground black pepper	*2 large cloves garlic, crushed*
grated nutmeg	*5 large tomatoes, sliced*
	2 oz (50 g) Cheddar cheese, grated

When the spinach is cool enough to handle, squeeze it thoroughly dry. Mix into the béchamel and season to taste with salt, pepper and nutmeg. Cover the bottom of a baking dish with the mixture. Toss the well-drained pasta with the olive oil and garlic and spread over the spinach layer. Arrange the tomato slices over the top, in slightly overlapping layers, and season well with salt and pepper. Sprinkle the grated cheese over the top. Bake at 180°C/350°F/gas 4 for 40–45 minutes or until nicely browned.

MACARONI SPECIAL

This version of the well-known macaroni cheese is light and creamy, and makes wholesome, satisfying family food. With the addition of mushrooms and leeks, it is almost a meal in itself, needing only some grilled tomatoes and, perhaps, the cauliflower salad on page 140.

FOR 4–6

8oz (250g) macaroni	6oz (175g) Cheddar cheese, grated
2 small leeks, shredded	
2 free-range eggs	sea salt and freshly ground black pepper
1 pint (600ml) skimmed or soya milk	grated nutmeg
1oz (25g) margarine, melted, or 2 tbs olive oil	6oz (175g) mushrooms, sliced

Put the macaroni into a large pan of boiling water with the shredded leeks and simmer for 5 minutes or until half cooked. Drain.

Whisk the eggs with the milk and add the melted margarine or oil and the grated cheese. Season with salt, pepper and nutmeg.

Put the macaroni and leeks into a baking dish. Cover with the sliced mushrooms. Pour the egg mixture over the top and bake at 180°C/350°F/gas 4 for 35–45 minutes or until the top is browned. Leave for 10 minutes before serving, to allow it to set in the centre and cool a little.

RICE NOODLES WITH BROCCOLI, GINGER AND GARLIC ᵛ

The combination of ginger and garlic gives a classic oriental flavour to this quick and easy supper dish. You can buy black bean sauce and dark sesame oil from oriental grocers – they are useful standbys to have on the larder shelf.

FOR 6

1lb (500g) rice vermicelli	1 inch (2.5cm) fresh root ginger, peeled and grated very finely
2½lb (1.25kg) broccoli florets	
	2-3 large cloves garlic, crushed
For the sauce:	3 tbs black bean sauce
4 spring onions, sliced very finely	1 tbs soy sauce or to taste
	6 tbs dark sesame oil

To make the sauce, mix all the ingredients together and leave to stand while you cook the broccoli and vermicelli.

Cover the rice vermicelli with cold water in a large saucepan. Bring to the boil, then remove from the heat and leave to soak for 5 minutes. Meanwhile, steam the broccoli florets and cut them small.

Drain the vermicelli thoroughly and toss with the broccoli florets and the prepared sauce.

SIMPLE SAFFRON RICE ♥

*S*affron yellow adds visual appeal to the flavour of the spices in this rice dish, and toasted cashew nuts provide a contrasting crunch.

FOR 4

6oz (175g) basmati rice	3oz (75g) frozen peas, thawed
2 tbs olive oil	pinch of saffron strands
2 fresh red chillies, deseeded and sliced very finely (optional)	soaked in 2 tbs water, drained
	sea salt
3 cardamom pods, split open	1 cinnamon stick, bruised
1-2 tsp cumin seeds	2oz (50g) cashew nuts, browned lightly under the grill

Rinse the rice and cook it until tender (see page 96). Meanwhile, heat the oil and toss the sliced chillies, cardamom pods and cumin seeds for about 2 minutes or until they give out their aromas.

Toss the spice mixture, peas and saffron into the drained hot rice and season with a little salt. Place the cinnamon stick in the centre and sprinkle the toasted cashew nuts over to garnish.

Saffron

It used to demand a price higher than gold – and is still an expensive spice. Saffron consists of the stamens of the saffron crocus, which have to be gathered manually, and picked out by hand. Powdered saffron is an adulterated form, merely a coloured and flavoured mixture. So where you can, use the tiny thread-like stamens – they are intensely strong and you need only two or three to flavour a large quantity of food.

CHINESE EGG FRIED RICE

*A*lthough this is the ideal dish to go with samosas or spring rolls, or a simple stir-fry, it also makes an excellent main course in its own right. It is full of interest and colour, and the strips of lightly cooked free-range egg are a delicious finishing touch.

FOR 6

1 tbs dark sesame oil	4oz (125g) mangetout, sliced diagonally
2 free-range eggs, beaten	
1 tbs vegetable oil	1 inch (2.5cm) root ginger, peeled and grated
4 spring onions, sliced finely	
1 yellow pepper, deseeded and diced small	2 large cloves garlic, chopped finely
1 medium carrot, cut into fine matchsticks	8oz (250g) long-grain rice, cooked (see page 96)
8oz (250g) canned water chestnuts, sliced	soy sauce
	paprika

Heat the sesame oil in a frying pan and pour in the beaten eggs. Stir a little until they set like a thin omelette, then flip over to cook the other side lightly. Turn out on to a wire rack and cool. Cut into thin strips.

Heat the vegetable oil in a wok until very hot. Stir-fry (see page 56) all the vegetables with the ginger and garlic for 3 minutes, then turn the heat down and cook for a further 3 minutes or until they are tender but still slightly crisp. Stir in the rice, mixing well, and season to taste with soy sauce and paprika. Finally, fold in the egg strips and it is ready to serve. Delicious with the sweet and sour sauce on page 153.

OPPOSITE: Simple Saffron Rice (top) and Chinese Egg Fried Rice with Sweet and Sour Sauce on the side

GREEK RICE WITH LEEKS ❤

This tasty dish of chilli-spiced rice simmered gently with leeks is topped with thick Greek yogurt (which vegans can omit, of course).

FOR 4

3 tbs olive oil	12 oz (350 g) leeks, sliced
2 medium onions, chopped roughly	sea salt and freshly ground black pepper
1 tsp chilli powder or to taste	thick plain Greek yogurt to serve (optional)
6 oz (175 g) long-grain rice	
½ pint (300 ml) vegetable stock or water	

Heat the olive oil in a medium saucepan and sauté the onions for 3–4 minutes or until they begin to soften. Add the chilli powder and the rinsed rice and stir well to coat the grains with oil. Pour in the vegetable stock or water, stirring, then add the sliced leeks and a little salt and pepper. Bring to the boil. Turn the heat down and simmer gently, covered with a lid, for 20–25 minutes or until the rice is cooked. Check the seasoning.

Heap a tablespoon of thick Greek yogurt on top of each serving.

PERSIAN CHILAU RICE ❤

An unusual way of cooking rice, this has a crunchy texture and is gently spiced.

FOR 4

6 oz (175 g) basmati rice	To garnish:
2 tsp ground cumin or to taste	thick plain Greek yogurt (optional)
sea salt	toasted flaked almonds
2 tbs olive oil	
1 oz (25 g) margarine	

How to Cook Rice

There is a simple ratio of 1 to 2 when cooking rice: to one measure of rice you add two measures of water. So weigh the amount of rice required in the recipe, and put it into a cup or measuring jug. You will need two of the cups or measuring jugs full of water to cook the rice.
1. Rinse rice before you cook it. Then put it into a saucepan, add the measured water and bring to the boil.
2. Turn the heat down and cover with a lid so that the pan is sealed. Leave the rice to cook, covered all the time, until it has absorbed all the water. This takes 8-10 minutes for white rice, or up to 20 minutes for brown or risotto rice.
3. Add some salt if you wish and fluff up the rice with a fork.

Par-cook the rinsed rice for 5 minutes, then drain thoroughly. Mix with the cumin and a little salt.

Heat the olive oil with half of the margarine in a heavy-bottomed saucepan. Pack the rice into the pan, smooth the surface and dot with the remaining margarine. Cover closely with foil. Cover the pan tightly with a lid and turn the heat right down. Cook over the lowest possible heat for 35–40 minutes or until the rice is completely tender and a golden-brown crust has formed on the base. Check the seasoning.

Spoon into a warm serving dish so that the crunchy golden bits are mingled with the soft rice, and top with a few spoonfuls of Greek yogurt, if using. Scatter toasted flaked almonds over the top and it is ready to serve.

MEXICAN RICE 'N' BEANS ⓥ

So easy to make, this is hot and tasty, an interesting alternative to beans on toast – and just as nutritious. Provide Tabasco sauce for those who like their Mexican food REALLY hot!

FOR 2–3

1 x 14oz (400g) can kidney bean or black beans, drained (or equivalent cooked dried, see page 185)

1 large onion, chopped

2 large cloves garlic, sliced

2oz (50g) margarine

1 tbs wholemeal flour

2 tsp ground cumin or to taste

½–1 tsp chilli powder

½ pint (300ml) vegetable stock

3oz (75g) long-grain rice, cooked (see opposite)

Tabasco sauce to hand around (optional)

In a saucepan mix the beans with the onion and garlic. Using a fork, mix the margarine, flour and spices to a paste. Pour the vegetable stock over the beans, add the spice paste and heat gently, stirring, until smoothly blended. Simmer, uncovered and stirring from time to time, for 30 minutes or until the sauce thickens like gravy.

Arrange the hot cooked rice around the edge of a shallow serving dish and pour the beans into the centre. Serve at once, with Tabasco to hand around.

SPANISH RICE ⓥ

Speed and simplicity are the keynotes here. The spicy vegetable mixture can be cooked in the time it takes to boil the rice. This is a dish likely to be a regular favourite at any time of the year.

FOR 4

1 large onion, sliced finely

2 tbs olive oil

3 stalks celery, sliced

6oz (175g) frozen peas, cooked and drained

1 fresh chilli, deseeded and sliced finely (to taste)

1 x 14oz (400g) can chopped tomatoes with juice, or 6 fresh tomatoes, skinned (see page 59) and chopped

garam masala

sea salt and freshly ground black pepper

6oz (175g) long-grain rice, cooked (see opposite)

Cook the onion in the oil over a gentle heat, covered with a lid and stirring occasionally, for 8–10 minutes or until softened.

Stir in the celery over a moderate heat, then add the peas and sliced chilli and mix in well. Heat through, then add the chopped tomatoes and cook for 5 minutes. Season to taste with garam masala, salt and pepper.

Stir into the hot cooked rice and it is ready to serve.

MUSHROOM RISOTTO

The delicate flavours of this risotto can be varied by adding chopped pumpkin or other vegetables. It is a delicious supper dish, perfect with a salad of mixed leaves dressed in the lemony caper vinaigrette on page 147.

FOR 4

1lb (500g) mixed mushrooms, eg chestnut, shiitake, flat, field etc, sliced	*2¼ pints (1.5 litres) hot vegetable stock*
4 tbs olive oil	*3oz (75g) cheese, grated*
2 cloves garlic, crushed	*1 tbs finely chopped fresh tarragon*
2 tbs chopped parsley	*ground mace*
1 onion, chopped	*sea salt and freshly ground black pepper*
6oz (175g) arborio or other risotto rice	

Sauté the mushrooms briskly for just a minute or so in 2 tbs of the olive oil, adding the crushed garlic and chopped parsley once the juices begin to run. Draw off the heat, cover with a lid and set aside.

Soften the onion in the rest of the oil over a gentle heat, covered, for 6–7 minutes. Then add the rice and stir until it is well coated with oil. Add a ladleful of the hot stock and simmer, stirring, until it has been absorbed, then add another ladleful of stock. Continue adding the stock a little at a time and simmering until the rice absorbs the liquid before adding more.

When all the stock has been added and the rice is fully cooked, stir in the cheese and tarragon. Season with mace, salt and pepper, fold in the mushrooms with all their juices, and serve.

Types of Rice

LONG GRAIN – is the most versatile and popular of all types and comes white or brown.

SHORT GRAIN – is often used for risottos and puddings and is usually white. If you can find brown short-grain rice, use it to make delicious, slightly more crunchy risottos.

BROWN RICE – is the best rice in nutritional terms: the whole natural grain still with its edible husk, which makes it high in dietary fibre. It has a delicious flavour and nutty texture. Brown rice, both long-grain and short-grain, needs a little more water and longer cooking than white rice.

BASMATI – is a narrow long-grain rice variety with a fabulous flavour, great with Indian food. It comes brown or white. Grown in India and Italy.

ARBORIO – from Italy, is a plump short-grain rice with good flavour. It makes excellent risottos.

'PUDDING' RICE – is polished short-grain rice that goes mushy when cooked because of its high starch content. Perfect for a creamy rice pudding.

WILD RICE – is not a true rice at all, but the seed of a water grass. It is long and narrow, grey-brown in colour and nutty in flavour. Wild rice requires longer cooking than other rice – 30-40 minutes – but is nice to mix into rice dishes for variety. I always add a handful of wild rice to long-grain rice.

RICE FLOUR – is a good thickening agent in sauces and stews, and can be used in baking. Invaluable for people with a gluten allergy.

OPPOSITE: Mushroom Risotto

VEGETARIAN MINCE AND RICE STIR-FRY ∨

*S*erve this quick supper dish with a green vegetable such as creamed spinach purée (see page 46), lemon green beans (see page 44) or a crunchy vegetable salad.

FOR 4

2 tbs olive oil	*1 tbs chopped fresh parsley or other herbs*
1 large onion, chopped finely	
6oz (175g) vegetarian mince	*1 tbsp tomato purée, or 1 x 8oz (250g) can chopped tomatoes*
6oz (175g) long-grain rice, cooked (see page 96)	*sea salt and freshly ground black pepper*

Heat the oil in a wok or frying pan and sauté the onion for 5 minutes. Add the mince and stir-fry for 5 minutes or until lightly browned. Stir in the rice, herbs and tomato purée or tomatoes. Season to taste. Heat through, stirring.

RICE AND VEGETABLE CHEESE BAKE

*M*ixed vegetables spiced with turmeric, cumin and ginger are folded into rice with cheese. The full flavour of this bake goes beautifully with the roasted pepper salad on page 139 or steamed green vegetables.

FOR 6

1 onion, sliced	*sea salt and freshly ground black pepper*
3 tbs olive oil	
3 courgettes, cubed	*8oz (250g) brown long-grain rice, cooked (see page 96)*
1 yellow pepper, deseeded and cut into small squares	*4oz (125g) Cheddar cheese, grated*
6oz (175g) sweetcorn	*2 free-range eggs, beaten*
1 tsp each turmeric, ground cumin and ground ginger or to taste	*1oz (25g) margarine*

Soften the onion in the oil for 5 minutes over a gentle heat, covered with a lid. Stir in the other vegetables and toss to mix, then cover the pan again and cook for about 10 minutes or until all the vegetables are tender, stirring from time to time. Stir in the spices and season with salt and pepper. Mix into the cooked rice with the grated cheese, and fold in the beaten eggs.

Spread the mixture in an ovenproof dish and dot the top with the margarine. Cover the dish with foil and bake at 180°C/350°F/gas 4 for 40–45 minutes. Allow to rest for 10 minutes before serving, with a cheese and parsley sauce (see page 155).

SHEPHERD'S PIE ❤

*N*othing can beat a good shepherd's pie. Making it with vegetarian mince is even better than the original version because it is lighter and less greasy. You can add other chopped vegetables to the mixture, such as courgettes, broccoli or leeks, and vary the dish each time you make it.

FOR 4–6

1½ lb (750 g) potatoes, peeled	*2 carrots, sliced thinly*
3 oz (75 g) margarine	*8 oz (250 g) vegetarian mince*
1-2 tbs skimmed or soya milk	*2 tbs soy sauce*
sea salt and freshly ground	*½ pint (300 ml) vegetable stock*
black pepper	*ground mace, grated nutmeg*
1 large onion, chopped	*or garam masala (optional)*

Cook the potatoes in boiling water for 20 minutes or until quite soft, then drain well and mash them with 2 oz (50 g) of the margarine and enough skimmed or soya milk to make a firm but smooth consistency. Season to taste.

Melt the remaining margarine in a frying pan and add the onion and carrots. Cover with a lid and cook for about 10 minutes or until soft, stirring occasionally. Add the vegetarian mince, soy sauce and vegetable stock. Bring to the boil and simmer gently, uncovered, for 8–10 minutes. Season to taste with salt and pepper and any spices of your choice.

Put the mince mixture into a baking dish and cover with the mashed potatoes. Bake at 200°C/400°F/gas 6 for 30 minutes or until the potato topping is well browned.

STUFFED BAKED POTATOES

A nice change from plain jacket baked potatoes. You can vary the vegetables you put in – chopped onions or leeks, sliced mushrooms, diced peppers, small broccoli florets and sweetcorn would all be delicious.

FOR 4–6

4 large baking potatoes, scrubbed	*4 oz (125 g) cooked peas*
	4 oz (125 g) cooked carrots, diced small
½ pint (300 ml) béchamel sauce (see page 155)	
4 oz (125 g) Cheddar cheese, grated, plus more for the tops	

Bake the potatoes at 200°C/400°F/gas 6 for 1¼ hours or until tender. Cut in half lengthwise and remove the flesh, being careful not to break the skins. Put the flesh in a bowl and set the skins aside.

Heat the béchamel gently and stir in the grated cheese until it melts. Add to the potato flesh and mash well, then fold in the prepared vegetables. Fill the potato skins with the mixture. Cover with more grated cheese and replace in the oven. Bake for a further 6–8 minutes or until the tops are lightly browned.

CREAMY POTATO AND LEEK BAKE

*L*ayers of thinly sliced potatoes and leeks, with a central layer of mushrooms flavoured with garlic and fresh herbs, are baked under a creamy topping with crisp crumbs.

FOR 2–3

2 large cloves garlic, crushed	12oz (350g) leeks, sliced
2 tbs olive oil	sea salt and freshly ground black pepper
8oz (250g) mushrooms, sliced	grated nutmeg
2 tbs chopped fresh herbs, eg thyme, tarragon and parsley, or 1½ tsp dried mixed herbs, plus more for the layers	6 fl oz (175ml) crème fraîche or single cream
	5 tbs skimmed or soya milk
12oz (350g) potatoes, peeled and sliced thinly	2oz (50g) fresh breadcrumbs
	1oz (25g) margarine

Sauté the garlic in the oil for 2 minutes, then add the mushrooms and herbs and toss together. Cover and cook gently for 5 minutes.

Layer half of the potatoes and leeks in an ovenproof dish and season with salt, pepper, nutmeg and a sprinkling of herbs. Spoon the mushrooms and all their juices over the top and cover with the rest of the leeks and potatoes. Spoon the crème fraîche or cream over the top and add the skimmed or soya milk. Cover tightly with foil and cook at 190°C/375°F/gas 5 for 1 hour.

Remove the foil. Sprinkle over the breadcrumbs, dot with the margarine and bake, uncovered, for 25–30 minutes or until the potatoes are tender.

POTATO AND AUBERGINE CURRY v

A beautifully spiced potato dish for cold weather. Serve with basmati rice, some naan bread, and shredded lettuce with the poppy seed dressing on page 146.

FOR 3–4

1 tsp chilli powder	1 fresh green chilli, deseeded and finely chopped
½ tsp turmeric	1 x 7oz (200g) can chopped tomatoes, or 3 large fresh tomatoes, skinned (see page 59) and chopped
2 tsp ground cumin or to taste	
1 tsp ground coriander or to taste	
1 tsp sea salt	4 medium potatoes, boiled and cut into cubes
1 tbs tomato purée	
4 tbs vegetable oil	6oz (175g) vegetarian steak chunks, browned in a little oil (optional)
1lb (500g) aubergines, sliced	
1-2 tsp cumin seeds	
1 inch (2.5cm) root ginger, peeled and grated	fresh coriander leaves to garnish

Mix the spices, salt and tomato purée with 1 tbs of the oil in a small bowl. Spread the spice mixture over the cut sides of the aubergine slices. Cut the slices into strips.

Heat the remaining oil in a frying pan and fry the cumin seeds until they begin to pop. Add the aubergines and grated ginger and turn the heat down. Cover and cook for 8 minutes, stirring once or twice.

Add the chopped chilli, tomatoes and potatoes with 3-4 tbs water and simmer very gently, covered tightly, for 15-20 minutes, stirring from time to time.

Add the browned steak chunks, if using, and mix well. Serve garnished with coriander leaves.

OPPOSITE: Potato and Aubergine Curry

SAUTÉ OF SWEET POTATOES ♥

Sweet potatoes are loaded with beta carotene. Boil them in the same way as ordinary potatoes, as in this recipe. You can also bake them in their jackets (they don't take as long as ordinary potatoes), roast them, or make them into chips to serve with soured cream.

FOR 2-3

4 medium sweet potatoes, peeled	4oz (125g) brown sugar
1½oz (40g) margarine	2 tbs chopped fresh parsley or chives
grated rind and juice of 1 orange	

Cook the sweet potatoes in boiling water for 10–15 minutes or until they are tender. Drain well. Slice them or cut into cubes.

Heat the margarine in a frying pan and add the sweet potatoes. Toss over a moderate heat until the potatoes are covered with margarine, then add the orange rind and juice, the sugar and herbs. Heat through, stirring and tossing, and serve immediately.

CRISPY POTATO SKINS ♥

These make a very healthy snack, a good alternative to potato crisps. You can serve them with the spicy chilli dip on page 156 or guacamole (see page 157), or any other favourite dip or salsa.

FOR 4

4 baking potatoes, scrubbed	sea salt
sunflower or grapeseed oil	

Bake the potatoes at 200°C/400°F/gas 6 for 1¼ hours or until tender. Alternatively, microwave them for 10 minutes on full power. Leave to cool a little, then cut in half and carefully scoop out the flesh (you can use this for mashed potato or shepherd's pie, see page 101). Cut each half skin into three wide strips and then into squares.

Heat some oil in a frying pan until it is very hot – when you drop the first potato skin into the oil it should immediately start to sizzle. Cook the skins quickly on both sides until golden and crisp. Drain on kitchen paper to absorb excess oil, sprinkle with a little salt, and they are ready to serve.

OPPOSITE: Sauté of Sweet Potatoes (left) and Crispy Potato Skins, with Green Herb Dip (see page 157)

POTATO AND CABBAGE MASH ⓥ

*H*ere is a traditional country dish devised just for cold, bleak winter weather.

FOR 3–4

1 lb (500g) boiled potatoes	*6 spring onions, sliced finely*
¼ pint (150ml) skimmed or soya milk	*pinch of grated nutmeg*
1 lb (500g) cooked green cabbage, chopped	*sea salt and freshly ground black pepper*
	melted margarine

Mash the potatoes with the milk, or blend them together in the food processor. Turn into a saucepan and reheat, stirring. Add the cabbage and spring onions and mix well. Season with nutmeg, salt and pepper. Heat through.

Put into a dish, or place piles of mash on each plate, and make a deep well in the centre. Fill the well with melted margarine and eat, dipping each forkful of mash into the margarine.

GARLIC MASHED POTATOES ⓥ

*G*arlic lovers, this is a sensational way of eating potatoes – and garlic! It is based on a simple Spanish sauce of pounded garlic and olive oil.

FOR 3–4

4 cloves garlic	*2 lb (1 kg) potatoes, freshly boiled*
½ tsp sea salt	
6 tbs olive oil	*freshly ground black pepper*
squeeze of lemon juice	

In a mortar pound the garlic to a fine paste with the salt. Add the oil in a slow stream, pounding all the time so that the sauce thickens. Add the lemon juice to thin out the sauce and season with more salt if necessary.

Mash the hot potatoes well, then gradually beat in the garlic oil with an electric mixer or whisk. Season with pepper, and serve.

SPICY BEAN JACKETS ⓥ

*A*n easy lunch or supper dish, this will be very popular with both children and adults. In cold weather, serve bowls of soup too – the pumpkin soup on page 20 would be especially nice.

FOR 2

2 baking potatoes, scrubbed	*1 x 14oz (400g) can baked beans*
1 tbs olive oil	
1 small onion, chopped	*2 tbs curry paste or to taste*

Bake the potatoes at 200°C/400°F/gas 6 for 1¼ hours or until tender. Alternatively, microwave them for 10 minutes on full power.

Heat the oil in a pan and sauté the onion for 5–6 minutes or until crisp and browned. In another pan, heat the baked beans with the curry paste.

Cut the potatoes in half lengthwise. Cut a deep cross in the flesh of each half and top with the spiced baked beans. Sprinkle with the browned onions and serve.

SAVOURY FRIED POTATO ⱽ

*T*his is a delicious way to use up left-over mash! You can vary the recipe with sautéed mushrooms, leeks or onions, or grated cheese.

FOR 2-4

1 lb (500 g) mashed potatoes	freshly ground black pepper
plain flour	vegetable oil
sea salt	margarine

Divide the mashed potatoes into 4 or 8 equal portions and shape each into a cake with floured hands. (If the potatoes are moist you will need to mix a bit of flour into them to help bind the cakes.) Season some flour and use to coat the cakes lightly.

Heat a mixture of oil and margarine in a frying pan and fry the cakes over a moderate heat until crisp and golden brown on both sides. Serve hot.

ROSTI ⱽ

*S*erve this as a supper dish with a Caesar salad (see page 133), or as a side dish.

FOR 4

2 lb (1 kg) potatoes, peeled	2 tbs olive oil
sea salt and freshly ground black pepper	1 oz (25 g) margarine

Grate the potatoes coarsely. Press dry between sheets of kitchen paper and season well.

Heat the oil with the margarine in a heavy-bottomed frying pan over a high heat. Add the potatoes and flatten into a cake. Turn the heat down, cover tightly with a lid and cook gently for 25–30 minutes or until the base of the rosti is crusty and browned and the top is tender.

To turn out, place a plate over the top of the pan and turn the pan over so that the rosti falls out on to the plate. Serve at once.

SCALLOPED POTATOES

*T*his simple potato dish is a classic that you can vary by using all kinds of herbs and vegetables in between the layers of potato.

FOR 3-4

1½ lb (750 g) potatoes, peeled and sliced very thinly	sea salt and paprika
3 oz (75 g) margarine	1 tsp Dijon mustard (optional)
4 tbs finely chopped fresh chives, spring onions or leeks	½ pint (300 ml) skimmed or soya milk
4 tbs finely diced red pepper (optional)	single cream (optional)
	1-2 oz (25-50 g) Cheddar cheese, grated

Make layers of the potatoes in a shallow baking dish, with tiny knobs of margarine, the chives, spring onions or leeks, and optional peppers between them. Sprinkle each layer with sea salt and paprika as you go. Mix the mustard with a little milk, then add to the rest of the milk, with some cream if you like. Pour over the top of the layered potatoes and sprinkle with the grated cheese.

Bake at 180°C/350°F/gas 4 for 1½ hours, covered with foil for the first 30 minutes.

CHAPTER FIVE

Pastry

There is something very special about the sight of a pastry dish. It looks so appetizing – crisp, golden brown and mouthwateringly light. Perhaps an element of surprise comes into the pleasure too, as the pastry conceals some masterly mixture which will only be revealed on the cutting into portions. The wonderful selection of recipes in this section demonstrates just how versatile pastry is. Quiches, strudels, puff pastry turnovers, pasties, pies and flans are all to be found here – plus the most popular 'pie' of all, the pizza.

Fortunately, with the manufacture of frozen pastry, a lot of the drudgery has been taken out of cooking with pastry. Excellent brands of puff pastry and shortcrust are available everywhere, and take only a matter of moments to roll out and cut. (Make sure to examine the ingredients for animal fat such as suet, or additives.) Pizza bases are easily obtainable too.

If, however, you want to make your own pastry, there are recipes on pages 178 and 179.

MUSHROOM FILO PIE

A dramatic pie which makes a perfect party piece, this dish is full of flavour and texture – the succulence of mushrooms, the crispness of wafer-thin filo pastry, and a hint of smooth rice. Serve with the roasted red pepper sauce on page 149 and with a garlicky watercress salad (see page 136) or the special rocket salad on page 129.

FOR 4–6

2 shallots, sliced finely	*2 cloves garlic, crushed*
3 tbs olive oil plus extra for the pastry	*3 tbs chopped parsley*
	2 tbs chopped fresh tarragon
1½ lb (750g) mixed mushrooms, eg chestnut, shiitake, oyster, common and flat, all thinly sliced in the food processor	*5 tbs crème fraîche or single cream*
	3 oz (75g) basmati rice, cooked (see page 96)
	6 oz (175g) filo pastry

Soften the shallots in 1 tbs of the oil, then add the rest of the oil and the thinly sliced mushrooms. Toss until the mushrooms are well coated with oil and beginning to heat through, then turn the heat down a little and cover with a lid. Cook gently for 6–8 minutes or until the mushrooms are tender but not soggy, stirring occasionally. Add the garlic and herbs and stir well, then stir in the crème fraîche or single cream off the heat. Finally mix in the cooked rice and leave to cool.

Oil an 8 inch (20 cm) shallow tin, either square or round. Layer half of the filo pastry sheets in the tin, letting the edges of the pastry hang over the side of the tin all around by several inches. Brush each layer with oil as you go along. Drain excess liquid from the mushroom mixture, then spread it in the centre of the tin. Fold the pastry edges into the centre. Continue making layers with the rest of the filo, brushing with oil as you go, and crumpling, creasing or twisting up the top sheets to make a pattern. Brush the top well with more olive oil.

Bake at 200°C/400°F/gas 6 for 30 minutes or until golden. Cut into wedges and serve.

SAVOURY VEGETABLE STRUDEL

*T*his sensational pastry roll encases lightly cooked vegetables which are bound together with melted cheese. For something so special it is delightfully simple to prepare, and naturally you can experiment by varying the vegetables.

FOR 4–6

1½ oz (40g) margarine, melted	*6oz (175g) goat's cheese, feta or Cheddar cheese, sliced or crumbled*
3 tbs olive oil	
ten 12 x 6 inch (30 x 15cm) sheets filo pastry	*sea salt and freshly ground black pepper*
8oz (250g) courgettes, steamed and sliced thinly	*1 tbs fresh thyme*
8oz (250g) broccoli, steamed and sliced	*1 tbs chopped fresh tarragon (optional)*
4oz (125g) French beans, steamed and cut in half	*1 free-range egg, beaten*
	flowers or herbs to garnish

Mix the melted margarine with the olive oil. Brush 5 of the filo pastry sheets with the mixture and stack them on top of each other.

Mix the prepared vegetables together with the cheese. Season with salt and pepper and add the thyme and tarragon (if using). Take half of the mixture and spread it over the surface of the stacked pastry, leaving a 2 inch (5 cm) margin clear all around. Fold the short edges in, and roll up from a long side like a Swiss roll. Brush the surface with beaten egg and place seam-side down on a well-greased baking tray. Repeat with the other half of the ingredients to make a second strudel.

Bake at 190°C/375°F/gas 5 for 30–40 minutes or until golden brown and crisp. Leave to stand for a few minutes before slicing, and serve on a warmed dish garnished with flowers or herbs.

VEGETABLE SPRING ROLLS ♥

*S*pring rolls are perennial favourites and the home-made variety is unbeatable. Serve these as a starter for a special meal, or as a supper dish for friends, with Chinese egg fried rice (see page 94).

MAKES 12

2 tbs groundnut or olive oil plus more for deep frying	*3oz (75g) beansprouts*
	4 spring onions, chopped finely
12oz (350g) mixed vegetables, such as mangetout, peas, broccoli, courgettes, carrots, water chestnuts, all cut very small	*2 inches (5cm) root ginger, peeled and grated*
	1 clove garlic, chopped finely
5oz (150g) button mushrooms, chopped	*2-3 tbs soy sauce*
	24 sheets filo pastry

Heat the groundnut oil and stir-fry (see page 56) all the prepared vegetables with the ginger and garlic. Stir in soy sauce to taste. Remove from the heat, cover and leave to stand for several minutes.

Put 2 tablespoons of the vegetable filling on a single filo sheet and roll it up, tucking in the sides to make a neat parcel. Immediately roll this roll in another sheet of filo. Repeat to make 12 spring rolls in all. Deep-fry in very hot oil (190°C/375°F), turning the spring rolls until they are light golden all over and crisp. Drain on kitchen paper and serve as soon as possible.

OPPOSITE: Savoury Vegetable Strudel

CREAMY VEGETABLE PIE

The joy of this pie is that you can make it across the seasons, choosing your favourite vegetables. Spring, summer or winter it makes a mouthwatering meal, served with noodles and the fennel salad on page 134.

FOR 4–6

8oz (250g) sweetcorn, fresh (see page 34 for stripping corn from cob) or canned	*½ pint (300ml) béchamel sauce (see page 155), made with ¼ pint (150ml) single cream and ¼ pint (150ml) milk*
12oz (350g) broccoli	*bunch of fresh summer herbs of your choice, eg tarragon, thyme, dill, chopped*
12oz (350g) courgettes	
12oz (350g) carrots	
4oz (125g) French beans	*8oz (250g) frozen or home-made puff pastry (see page 178)*
3 small leeks	

Steam all the vegetables separately until they are tender but still slightly crisp. Alternatively, cook them in the microwave. Leave to cool, reserving cooking liquids, then chop if necessary into bite-size pieces.

Thin out the béchamel with about ¼ pint (150 ml) of the reserved liquids. Stir in the vegetables and herbs and pour into a large ovenproof dish.

Roll out the pastry to a round or other shape that is 1 inch (2.5 cm) larger than the diameter of the dish. With the trimmings make a long thin strip of pastry. Moisten the rim of the dish and place this strip on it. Moisten the strip, then place the pastry lid on top and press down with a fork to seal the edge.

Bake at 200°C/400°F/gas 6 for 30–40 minutes or until the pastry is risen and golden.

CLASSIC PASTIES ˅

Nothing could be easier or cheaper than these tasty pasties. Made in the classic way, they need a lot of tomato sauce to go with them, and are a very satisfying supper dish.

MAKES 4

6oz (175g) vegetarian mince	*1 lb (500g) easy shortcrust pastry (see page 179)*
4oz (125g) each potato, turnip and carrot, all grated finely	*4 tbs water*
sea salt and freshly ground black pepper	*milk*

Mix the vegetarian mince with the grated vegetables and season with salt and pepper. Roll out the pastry and cut into four 8 inch (20 cm) circles, or you can make 8 little pasties, using 5 inch (12.5 cm) circles. Divide the mince mixture among the circles, placing it in a heap in the centre. Add ½–1 tbs water to each. Moisten the pastry edges, then fold over into half-moon shapes. Press the edges together, turn them and crimp with a fork to make sure they are well sealed. Brush with milk and place on a well-greased baking tray.

Bake at 220°C/425°F/gas 7 for 10 minutes, then turn the heat down to 180°C/350°F/gas 4 and bake for a further 15 minutes. Cool a little on a rack, then lift carefully off the baking tray to serve.

LIGHT SPINACH AND CHEESE PIE

*T*his traditional pie makes a delicious meal served with scalloped potatoes (see page 107) and courgettes with sweetcorn (page 43). Good, honest, country food.

FOR 4

1 onion, chopped	*sea salt and freshly ground*
1 tbs olive oil	*black pepper*
1½ lb (750g) cooked spinach,	*grated nutmeg*
well drained and chopped	*9 oz (275g) easy shortcrust*
¼ pint (150 ml) béchamel	*pastry (see page 179)*
sauce (see page 155)	*1 free-range egg yolk, beaten*
4 oz (125g) Caerphilly cheese,	
grated	

Soften the onion in the oil for 5–6 minutes, covered with a lid. Add the spinach and mix well, then stir in the béchamel. Mix in the grated cheese. Season with salt, pepper and nutmeg. Set aside.

Roll out 5 oz (150g) of the pastry dough and line a greased 8 inch (20 cm) round tin, leaving a raised rim around the edge. Pour the spinach filling into the pastry case. Roll out the rest of the pastry dough into a round ½ inch (1 cm) larger in diameter than the top of the tin. Moisten the bottom pastry rim, place the top carefully over it and crimp the edges together tightly. Press them down with a fork to seal. Brush the top with beaten egg yolk.

Bake at 200°C/400°F/gas 6 for 30–35 minutes or until the pastry is golden. Serve hot or warm.

BEST VEGETABLE QUICHE

A quiche is always a winner – a crisp pastry case holding a lovely creamy vegetable filling. The version here uses courgettes. Alternative vegetables include: broccoli florets, sliced or small button mushrooms, thinly sliced leeks, chopped artichoke hearts, cauliflower florets and spinach. Quiches freeze well, so can be a useful standby.

FOR 6

9 oz (275g) easy shortcrust	*2 tsp garam masala or to taste*
pastry (see page 179)	*(optional)*
1¼ lb (625g) small courgettes,	*3 free-range eggs*
sliced thinly	*7 fl oz (200 ml) single cream*
2 oz (50g) margarine	*sea salt*
2 large cloves garlic, sliced	
finely	

Roll out the pastry dough and line a greased 8 inch (20 cm) loose-bottomed flan tin. Bake blind until part cooked (see page 115). Leave to cool.

Sauté the courgettes in the margarine until soft and turning golden brown. Remove from the heat and mix in the garlic and optional garam masala. Beat the eggs thoroughly with the cream and season with a little salt.

Arrange the courgettes in overlapping rings in the pastry case, then carefully pour the cream and egg mixture over the top. Bake at 220°C/425°F/gas 7 for 30 minutes. Cool on a wire rack for at least 10 minutes before lifting the quiche carefully out of the tin.

Pastry

CHEESE AND BROCCOLI TART

This distinctive tart, with the tangy flavour of goat's cheese, makes a memorable lunch, or is excellent on a picnic. You can use ricotta or Cheddar if you prefer a softer taste, and you can substitute cauliflower for broccoli as a variation.

FOR 6

9oz (275g) easy shortcrust pastry (see page 179)	4oz (125g) goat's cheese, sliced
1 large onion, chopped	4 free-range eggs
1 tbs olive oil	¼ pint (150ml) skimmed milk or single cream
12oz (350g) broccoli florets	3-4 tbs skimmed or soya milk
sea salt and freshly ground black pepper	

Roll out the pastry dough and line a greased 9–10 inch (22.5–25cm) loose-bottomed flan tin. Bake blind until part cooked.

Soften the onion in the oil, covered with a lid, for 5 minutes. Steam the broccoli florets for 5–6 minutes or until tender but still slightly crisp. Mix them with the onion and season with salt and pepper. Spread in the bottom of the cooked pastry case and intersperse with the slices of cheese.

Beat the eggs thoroughly and stir in the milk or cream plus the extra milk. Season to taste with salt and pepper. Pour over the broccoli. Bake at 200°C/400°F/gas 6 for 30 minutes or until lightly browned and set. Serve hot or warm.

Baking Blind

Baking blind means baking a pastry case before it is filled. If after the filling is put in, the tart, quiche, flan, etc is to be baked further, then the pastry case is baked blind only until it is part cooked. If no further baking is to be done after the filling is added, the pastry case is baked blind until it is completely cooked.

Roll out the pastry dough on a lightly floured board and line the tin. Press the dough lightly into the corners and edges, and trim the edge. Prick with a fork in several places, then spread a piece of foil smoothly over bottom and sides of the pastry case; the foil should overlap the rim of the tin by 2 inches (5cm). Fill with baking beans. (You can buy ceramic baking beans, or simply use dried beans that you keep for this use alone – once baked they cannot be cooked.)

Bake at 200°C/400°F/gas 6 for 10-15 minutes or until just set, then remove the beans and foil. Return to the oven (without the foil and beans) and bake for a further 5 minutes to crisp and brown the pastry slightly. The pastry case is now part cooked. To bake completely, return to the oven (without the foil and beans) and bake for a further 15 minutes or until the pastry is firm and golden brown.

OPPOSITE: Cheese and Broccoli Tart

VEGETABLE MILLE-FEUILLES WITH PESTO

*M*ille-feuilles don't necessarily have to be the domain of sweet pâtisserie – savoury ones are wonderful too: elegant, appetizing food that melts in the mouth.

FOR 4

1 lb (500 g) frozen or home-made puff pastry (see page 178)	*For the vegetable filling:*
	1½ lb (750 g) mixed vegetables, eg asparagus, mangetout, broccoli florets, peas, courgettes, sweetcorn, spinach
1 free-range egg, beaten	*7 fl oz (200 ml) crème fraîche*
	2 tbs pesto sauce (see page 149)

Roll the pastry out thinly and cut it into 8 rectangles measuring 2 x 5 inches (5 x 12.5 cm). Brush each one with beaten egg and place on a well-greased baking tray. Bake at 200°C/400°F/gas 6 for 8–10 minutes or until well risen and golden. Split the pastry puffs horizontally about one-third of the way up their height, and keep hot.

Cut the vegetables into short lengths or small cubes and steam them until they are tender but still crisp. Mix together the crème fraîche and pesto and fold in the vegetables so that they are lightly coated. Heat through gently.

Pile the vegetable filling on the bottom layer of each mille-feuille and cover with the top layer of pastry. Serve immediately.

EASY LEEK PUFFS

*Y*ou can vary the filling for these delectably light puff pastry triangles throughout the seasons – broccoli, courgettes, peas, spinach and mushrooms all make tasty fillings. They are wonderfully easy to make, and a firm favourite whenever they appear.

MAKES 4

12 oz (350 g) leeks, chopped and cooked	*1 lb (500 g) frozen or home-made puff pastry (see page 178)*
½ pint (300 ml) béchamel sauce (see page 155)	*1 free-range egg yolk, beaten*
1 oz (25 g) Cheddar cheese, grated	

Stir the leeks into the béchamel, mixing thoroughly. Stir in the grated cheese.

Roll out the puff pastry fairly thinly and cut it into four 5 inch (12.5 cm) squares. Moisten the edges with water. Place one-quarter of the leek mixture in the centre of each square. Take one corner and fold it over to the opposite corner. Press the edges of the triangle together with a fork, so that they are well sealed. Brush the tops with beaten egg yolk and place on a well-greased baking tray.

Bake at 220°C/425°F/gas 7 for 20–25 minutes or until risen and golden.

EASY PIZZA

A home-made pizza is hard to beat, and makes a satisfying and delicious meal for all the family. Serve with a simple leafy salad tossed with the garlic mustard dressing on page 146.

FOR 4

For the dough:	For the topping:
scant ¼ oz (5g) easy-blend yeast	6 tsp tomato purée
10 oz (300g) plain flour	12 oz (350g) ripe tomatoes, sliced
pinch of salt	1 tbs mixed dried herbs
4-5 fl oz (125-150 ml) warm water	sea salt and freshly ground black pepper
1 tbs olive oil	optional garnishes: sliced fresh chilli, red onion rings, black olives
	6 oz (175g) mozzarella cheese, sliced, or firm goat's cheese, grated

To make the dough, mix the yeast with the flour and salt, and stir in enough warm water to make a soft dough. Knead thoroughly for 10–15 minutes. Halfway through this time, add the olive oil.

Press out the dough in a well-greased 11 inch (27.5 cm) metal pizza plate. Cover with a cloth and leave to rise in a warm place for 1 hour.

Spread the tomato purée over the dough and arrange the tomato slices on top. Sprinkle with the herbs, and season with salt and pepper. If you are using chilli or red onion rings, scatter them on top. Cover with the cheese and add olives, if using.

Bake at 220°C/425°F/gas 7 for 20–25 minutes or until the base is well cooked and the topping browned.

OTHER IDEAS FOR TOPPINGS

- red onions, blue cheese and rosemary
- grilled aubergines and simple pesto **v**
- leeks, tomatoes and goat's cheese
- roasted aubergines and mozzarella
- multicolour peppers, tomatoes and mozzarella
- wild mushrooms, garlic and herbs **v**
- artichoke hearts, onions and cheese

CHAPTER SIX

Barbecues

Usually people associate barbecues with a lot of meat, but now that meat analogues are so good, and so widely available, even the most committed of carnivores will enjoy a meatless barbecue. You can grill vegetarian sausages, you can skewer vegetarian steak chunks on to mixed vegetable kebabs, and you can grill meatless patties and other products that come straight from your larder to the hot coals. I usually coat veggie burgers, hot dogs and so on with my tasty barbecue sauce. You can't beat it!

There are plenty of vegetables that barbecue very successfully – aubergine cooks beautifully over hot coals, as do courgettes, mushrooms and potatoes. Corn on the cob is wonderful. You can marinate all of these in barbecue sauce, or just brush them with olive oil, and they are mouthwatering. Grilled halloumi cheese is irresistible too.

Serve these with a tempting variety of salads (see pages 128 to 147 for ideas) and lots of tasty sauces, home-made salsas and dips (pages 149 to 157).

MARINATED VEGETARIAN SAUSAGES AND BURGERS ᵛ

*M*y piquant, garlicky barbecue sauce is perfect for brushing on to vegetarian sausages and burgers before cooking. For extra flavour, make your fire with mesquite or other aromatic woods, or use a good charcoal.

FOR 6–8

vegetarian sausages and burgers	*buns or baps to serve*
barbecue sauce (see page 153)	

Brush the sausages and burgers with barbecue sauce and, unless you are using frozen ones, leave to marinate if you have the time.

When the fire is ready, put your sausages and burgers on the grill and brown them, then flip them over and brown the other side. Vegetarian burgers and sausages don't need as long to cook as meat because they are not so tough!

Serve in buns or baps with more barbecue sauce or with any other goodie from this section or others.

VEGETABLE KEBABS ᵛ

*C*olourful combinations of vegetables make beautiful kebabs, which you can vary endlessly using peppers of all colours, tomatoes, courgettes etc – whatever is in high season. The kebabs are delicious with barbecued veggie burgers and a potato salad (see page 130). Serve with a variety of sauces such as barbecue (page 153), chilli (page 152), wild mushroom (page 154) or roasted red pepper (page 149).

FOR 6–8

8oz (250g) medium carrots, cut into chunks	*3 small corn cobs, cut across into 1 inch (2.5cm) slices*
1 small cauliflower, separated into florets	*milk or soya milk*
6oz (175g) mangetout, topped and tailed	*vegetarian sausages, burgers, grills etc, cut into chunks (optional)*
6oz (175g) baby onions, peeled	*olive oil*

Cook all the vegetables separately in boiling water to which you have added 1 tbs milk, until they are tender but still slightly crisp. Drain in a colander under cold running water.

Thread the pieces of vegetable on to skewers, alternating the colours. Include the chunks of vegetarian sausages, etc if you are using them. Brush with oil, and grill on the rack over hot coals for 5 minutes, turning frequently.

CHAR-GRILLED MUSHROOMS WITH ROSEMARY AND GARLIC ⱽ

Mushrooms take on the woody flavour of charcoal exceptionally well, and are always popular as part of a barbecue meal. I've used fresh shiitake mushrooms here, but you could just as easily substitute large button mushrooms

FOR 3–4

8oz (250g) shiitake mushrooms	1 tsp finely chopped fresh rosemary or ½ tsp dried rosemary
1 tbs olive oil	
1 tbs soy sauce	freshly ground black pepper
3 cloves garlic, crushed	

Trim the mushroom stalks. Mix the remaining ingredients together, add the mushrooms and toss to coat. Leave to marinate for up to 30 minutes.

Grill on the rack over hot coals for about 3 minutes on each side, and serve hot.

GRILLED MARINATED VEGETABLES ⱽ

Barbecued vegetables are scrumptious, particularly when they are marinated in this Japanese sauce which you can buy in bottles from most large supermarkets. You can also just brush the vegetables with plenty of olive oil before grilling them.

FOR 6

6 large flat mushrooms	¼ pint (150ml) teriyaki sauce
3 peppers	1 clove garlic, crushed
6 courgettes, cut in half lengthwise	4-5 fresh basil leaves, chopped, or a large pinch of chopped fresh tarragon
2 red onions, sliced thickly	

Cut the vegetables into bite-size pieces and thread them on to skewers, alternating the colours. Mix the teriyaki sauce with the garlic and basil or tarragon, add the skewers and leave to marinate for 20–30 minutes.

Put the skewers on the rack over hot coals and grill for about 5 minutes, turning from time to time.

GRILLED NUT-TOPPED TOMATOES

These juicy tomatoes, covered with a layer of herbs, nuts and cheese, make a delicious accompaniment to barbecued vegetarian sausages or burgers. The rocket and spinach salad on page 129 will complete the feast.

FOR 4 or 8

4 beef or large tomatoes	2 tbs grated cheese, preferably Parmesan
sea salt and freshly ground black pepper	3oz (75g) roasted peanuts, almonds or other nuts of choice, ground finely
soy sauce	margarine
1 tbs chopped fresh basil or tarragon	
1 tbs chopped parsley	

Cut the tomatoes in half crosswise and season the cut surfaces with salt and pepper. Sprinkle each half with a few drops of soy sauce. Mix the chopped basil or tarragon and parsley together and place on top, then sprinkle with the cheese. Cover with the ground nuts, patting on gently, and top each half with a small knob of margarine.

Wrap loosely in foil and place cut side up on the barbecue rack over hot coals. Grill for 20–25 minutes or until the tomatoes are soft and hot.

CHAR-GRILLED AUBERGINES ᵥ

Slices of aubergine marinated in herbs and oil take on the flavour of charcoal really well. They turn very soft and are wonderful with crisp barbecued vegetarian sausages and the avocado, mozzarella and tomato salad on page 134.

FOR 6

2 large aubergines	sea salt and freshly ground black pepper
olive oil	
chopped fresh herbs	

Cut the aubergines diagonally into ½ inch (1 cm) slices. Mix the olive oil with herbs, salt and pepper and brush over the cut sides of the aubergine slices. Leave to marinate for up to 1 hour, basting and turning occasionally.

Grill on the rack over hot coals for about 5–6 minutes on each side, until the aubergine is soft and well cooked.

Serve with sauces of your choice (see pages 149 to 153).

NEXT SPREAD: Vegetarian burgers and sausages with (clockwise from top left) Special Rocket Salad with Spinach and Parmesan, Balsamic Garlic and Herb Dressing, Chilli Sauce, Barbecue Sauce, bread rolls, Char-grilled Aubergines and Courgettes with Herbs, Char-grilled Mushrooms, Vegetable Kebabs, Sage and Cream Jackets and char-grilled corn on the cob

COURGETTES WITH HERBS ❧

Small courgettes marinated with herbs, garlic and ginger give out wonderful aromas as they are basted on the barbecue. They go beautifully with barbecued vegetarian sausages, and the watercress salad with garlic croutons on page 136.

FOR 8

8 small courgettes, trimmed	*2 dried bay leaves, crumbled*
2 cloves garlic, crushed	*4 tbs fresh lemon juice*
1 tbs grated fresh ginger	*3 tbs olive oil*
6 fresh mint leaves, chopped finely	*salt*
1 tsp chopped fresh marjoram	*lemon slices and sprigs of fresh herbs to garnish*
1 tsp chopped fresh lemon verbena or lemon balm	

Run the tip of a sharp knife along the courgettes to score them.

Mix the garlic, ginger and herbs with the lemon juice and oil and season with a little salt. Turn the courgettes in the mixture until thoroughly coated, then leave to marinate for 4–5 hours, turning occasionally.

Remove the courgettes from the marinade and grill on the rack over hot coals for 8–10 minutes or until tender but still 'al dente'. Turn and baste with the marinade frequently.

Serve skewered on wooden sticks, garnished with lemon slices and sprigs of fresh herbs.

SAGE AND CREAM JACKETS

Potatoes baked in foil, nestled in the hot coals, have a quality all their own, and topping them with this sage-flavoured soured cream sauce makes them even more delectable. Brilliant with char-grilled vegetarian sausages plus a couple of salads such as the green bean salad on page 141 and carrot salad on page 134. If you like, you can substitute chives for the sage.

FOR 6

6 baking potatoes, scrubbed	*1 tbs mild mustard*
olive oil	*sea salt and freshly ground black pepper*
3 tbs white wine vinegar	*¼ pint (150 ml) soured cream*
1 bunch spring onions, sliced finely	*1 tbs finely chopped fresh sage*
1 free-range egg yolk	*fresh sage leaves to garnish*

Rub the potatoes with oil and wrap in double thickness foil. Bake in the hot coals for 45 minutes to 1 hour or until soft, turning occasionally.

To make the sauce, put the vinegar into a small saucepan with the spring onions and cook gently until the vinegar has almost evaporated. Remove the pan from the heat. Beat together the egg yolk, mustard, salt and pepper, and stir into the spring onions. The mixture will thicken immediately. Stir in the soured cream and chopped sage and mix well. Keep hot.

Cut a deep cross in the top of each baked potato and squeeze the sides to open them out. Spoon in some sauce and serve garnished with sage leaves.

COUNTRY MUSHROOMS ▾

The rustic flavour of horseradish in the marinade permeates the mushrooms in this very simple recipe. Great as part of a large mixed barbecue menu along with vegetable kebabs (see page 119), sage and cream jackets (page 124) and a selection of salads and sauces.

FOR 6 or 12

¼ pint (150 ml) virgin olive oil	*12 flat mushrooms, stalks removed*
4 tbs horseradish sauce	
sea salt and freshly ground black pepper	*chopped parsley to garnish*

Mix together the olive oil and horseradish sauce in a soup plate or shallow dish and season to taste. Add the mushrooms and spoon the liquid over them until they are completely coated. Leave to marinate for a minimum of 30 minutes, basting occasionally.

Grill on the rack over hot coals for about 10 minutes, turning and basting occasionally. Garnish the open sides of the mushrooms with chopped parsley before serving.

CRUSTY GARLIC POTATOES

New potatoes stuffed with slivers of garlic and char-grilled with a crust of cornmeal make a very tasty dish to go with barbecued vegetarian burgers and a Caesar salad (see page 133). Delicious with the chilli sauce on page 152.

FOR 4-6

1 lb (500 g) new potatoes, scrubbed	*2 free-range eggs, beaten*
	6-8 tbs yellow cornmeal
3-4 large cloves garlic, peeled	*sprigs of parsley to garnish*

Cook the potatoes in boiling salted water for 12–15 minutes or until tender. Drain and leave to cool slightly. Slice the garlic thickly and, using the tip of a sharp knife or skewer, insert deeply into the potatoes. Dip the potatoes first into beaten egg and then in cornmeal to coat all over.

Grill on the rack over hot coals for 10–15 minutes or until crusty and golden, turning occasionally and taking care that the cornmeal doesn't burn. Serve in a basket lined with a clean napkin, garnished with sprigs of parsley.

PEACHES AND BUTTERSCOTCH

These make an irresistible finale to a barbecue party – peaches filled with ground almonds, baked over the coals and served with a creamy butterscotch sauce.

FOR 6 or 12

6 peaches, cut in half and stone removed	For the butterscotch sauce:
2 oz (50 g) ground almonds	3 oz (75 g) light soft brown sugar
	¼ pint (150 ml) maple syrup
	1½ oz (40 g) margarine
	pinch of salt
	¼ pint (150 ml) single cream
	1 tsp vanilla essence

To make the sauce, combine the sugar, maple syrup, margarine and salt in a heavy-bottomed saucepan. Bring to the boil, stirring to dissolve the sugar, and boil for 3 minutes or until the mixture is thick. Stir in the cream and bring back to the boil, then remove from the heat immediately and stir in the vanilla. Set aside.

Put the peach halves, cut side down, on squares of double thickness foil. Curl the edges of the foil up around the fruit and place on the rack over hot coals. Cook for 5 minutes.

Turn the peach halves over on the foil and spoon the ground almonds into the hollows. Pour 1 tbs of the butterscotch sauce over each half. Carefully draw up the edges of the foil over the top, and seal. Cook over the coals for a further 10 minutes or until tender. Serve hot with the remaining butterscotch sauce.

PRALINE BANANAS

Barbecuing bananas in their skins is a revelation. You can cook them over the coals very simply, with no extras, and serve them with whipped cream or ice cream. Or you can split the skins, insert slices of plain chocolate and heat over the coals until it melts. Here, crunchy praline is added, to devastating effect.

FOR 6

½ oz (15 g) shelled almonds	2 oz (50 g) granulated sugar
½ oz (15 g) shelled hazelnuts	6 under-ripe bananas

Put the nuts and sugar in a small heavy-bottomed frying pan and heat gently, stirring until the sugar dissolves. Turn the heat up and cook to a deep brown syrup. Immediately pour on to a sheet of non-stick paper placed on a metal baking sheet on a wooden board. Leave until cold and brittle, then crush finely.

Lay the unpeeled bananas flat and make a slit in the skin along the top. Slightly open out the skin and add about 1 tbs praline to each banana. Wrap up tightly in double-thickness foil and seal along the top. Cook directly on medium-hot coals for 8–10 minutes, turning halfway through the cooking time. Serve in the skins, with whipped cream or thick Greek yogurt.

OPPOSITE: Peaches and Butterscotch

CHAPTER SEVEN

Salads

*E*ating fresh, raw ingredients has been shown to be very beneficial to health, and is recommended as part of the daily diet. You can eat salads as main meals, as starters or as a side dish to go with a cooked meal. Full of vitamins and minerals, which are sometimes reduced or destroyed with cooking, salads give us a feeling of vitality and energy that many other foods do not.

A salad can be an art-form. The colours, textures and shapes of the kaleidoscope of ingredients combine to make endless pleasures for the table. Peppers come in yellow, red, orange, green, cream and even purple. The cream or very pale green of cauliflower next to the dark green spinach leaf; the russet of red-leaved lettuces alongside fresh greenery; baby carrots, sun-dried tomatoes, raw mushrooms, pulses of all colours, deep red beetroot – all these make up the palette for the artistic cook.

SUN-DRIED TOMATO AND CHICK PEA SALAD ❧

A garlicky dressing and the sweet-sharpness of cooked red onion in vinegar give this unusual salad memorable qualities. Serve with warm pitta bread as a light lunch dish or a starter.

FOR 4–6

½ small red onion, chopped finely	1 x 14 oz (400 g) can chick peas, drained (or equivalent cooked dried, see page 185)
1 tbs white wine vinegar	
4 tbs red wine vinegar	2 oz (50 g) sun-dried tomatoes in oil, diced
1 clove garlic, chopped finely	
sea salt and freshly ground black pepper	2 tbs chopped fresh parsley or tarragon
2 tbs extra virgin olive oil	2 tbs fresh lemon juice

Bring a small saucepan of water to the boil, add the onion and cook for 30 seconds. Drain, and toss with the white wine vinegar.

Mix together with the red wine vinegar, garlic, salt and pepper and gradually whisk in the oil. Toss the chick peas, sun-dried tomatoes and onion with the dressing and leave to marinate for 1 hour.

Add the chopped parsley or tarragon and lemon juice, toss to mix and serve at room temperature.

SPECIAL ROCKET SALAD WITH SPINACH AND PARMESAN

A salad of assertive flavours, this mixture of rocket and spinach in a simple dressing of olive oil and lemon juice makes a wonderful side dish or starter. Cheese shavings scattered over the top give added distinction.

FOR 2–3

5 oz (150 g) rocket leaves	2 tbs fresh lemon juice, or to taste
6 oz (175 g) young spinach leaves	
sea salt	1½ oz (40 g) Parmesan or any favourite cheese, finely shaved or grated
4 tbs extra virgin olive oil	

Prepare the rocket and spinach leaves, put them in a salad bowl and sprinkle with sea salt. Mix the olive oil with the lemon juice, add to the leaves and toss to coat. Scatter the shavings of Parmesan on top and it is ready to serve.

POTATO AND COS LETTUCE WITH GARLIC VINAIGRETTE ♥

The slightly bitter flavour of cos lettuce goes beautifully with the bland delicacy of potato, in a delicious garlicky dressing. Chopped chives are a perfect finishing touch

FOR 4–6

2 large cloves garlic, crushed	*1 cos lettuce, shredded coarsely*
5 tbs vinaigrette (see page 146)	*1 small red onion, chopped*
2 lb (1 kg) new potatoes, scrubbed	*finely*
	chopped chives to garnish

Stir the crushed garlic into the vinaigrette and leave to stand while you prepare the rest.

Cook the potatoes in boiling salted water until just tender but still firm in the centre. Drain, and rinse under cold water. Leave to cool, then cut into small cubes or slices.

Combine the potatoes, shredded cos and chopped onion in a salad bowl. Toss with the vinaigrette until well mixed and leave to stand for 20–30 minutes. Scatter chopped chives over the top just before serving.

POTATO SALAD

A delectable salad for all seasons: waxy potatoes, crunchy celery plus some spring onions in a lemony mayonnaise scented with dill and parsley.

FOR 4

1½ lb (750 g) small waxy potatoes, peeled, or new potatoes, scrubbed	*large handful of fresh dill, chopped*
4 stalks celery, chopped	*small bunch of parsley, chopped*
6 spring onions, sliced finely	*1 dill-pickled cucumber, chopped (optional)*
2-3 tbs fresh lemon juice	
5 tbs bottled or home-made mayonnaise (see page 150)	

Cook the potatoes in boiling salted water until just tender but still firm in the centre. Cool, and cut into cubes. Mix with the celery and spring onions.

Add lemon juice to the mayonnaise, flavouring it so that it is quite sharp. Stir in the chopped dill and mix thoroughly. Toss the potatoes in the dressing until well coated.

Put into a salad bowl and garnish with chopped parsley and dill-pickled cucumber (if using).

OPPOSITE: Potato and Cos Lettuce with Garlic Vinaigrette

WARM GOAT'S CHEESE SALAD

*T*his salad makes a lovely starter for a summer meal, especially served with hot garlic bread. Many goat's cheeses are made without the use of animal rennet, and will say so on the packet.

FOR 4

1 crisp lettuce	*4 sun-dried tomatoes in oil, sliced finely*
2oz (50g) fresh young spinach leaves	*1 tbs chopped mild onion*
1 bunch of watercress	*6oz (175g) creamy goat's cheese*
a handful of small radicchio leaves	*olive oil*
3 tbs vinaigrette (see page 146)	

Prepare all the salad leaves and toss them in the vinaigrette with the sun-dried tomatoes and onion. Divide among four plates. Slice the goat's cheese into rounds and brush them with olive oil. Grill until they blister and turn slightly golden, then place on top of the salads and serve immediately, with warm French bread.

Keeping Salad Fresh

Cut or torn salad leaves, washed and dried in a salad spinner, will keep crisp longer if they are stored in an airtight bag in the refrigerator.

CAESAR SALAD

*D*eservedly a classic, Caesar salad can be served as a starter or side dish, particularly with barbecues in high summer. It can be a light meal in itself, too, with just some warm wholemeal bread.

FOR 4

3 slices of bread, crusts removed	For the dressing:
oil for frying	*2 tbs balsamic vinegar*
1 large crisp lettuce, preferably cos	*1 tbs fresh lemon juice*
3oz (75g) lamb's lettuce	*1 tbs Dijon mustard*
8 spring onions, trimmed	*4 tbs extra virgin olive oil*
3 tbs finely grated cheese	*1 large clove garlic, crushed (optional)*

Cut the bread into small cubes and fry in hot oil until crisp and golden all over. Drain and cool on kitchen paper. Mix together the ingredients for the dressing.

Divide the lettuce into leaves and tear larger leaves into manageable pieces. Put into a bowl with the lamb's lettuce and spring onions and sprinkle the cheese over the top. Toss with the dressing and fold the croutons in just before serving.

OPPOSITE: Warm Goat's Cheese Salad

CARROT SALAD ♥

This salad is utterly simple, yet delicious, nutritious and fresh. If you prefer a slightly stronger bite, you can use a red onion instead of the spring onions.

FOR 4

8 medium carrots, grated	7 spring onions, chopped finely
4 tbs chopped parsley	3 tbs vinaigrette (see page 146)

Mix together the carrots, parsley and spring onions in a salad bowl. Dress with the vinaigrette and mix thoroughly.

FENNEL SALAD

This healthy, crunchy salad of fennel, carrot, apple and radish is dressed in a lemony mayonnaise, which adds to its freshness. Food for vitality.

FOR 4–6

12 radishes, trimmed	1 tbs fresh lemon juice
3 bulbs fennel, trimmed	6 tbs bottled or home-made
2 medium carrots, peeled	mayonnaise (see page 150)
1 green eating apple, cored	

Make four vertical cuts, crossing in the centre, in each radish. Soak in iced water for 2–3 hours or until the 'petals' open. Drain.

Cut the fennel bulbs lengthwise in half and cut out the hard core. Slice very finely. Cut the carrots into matchsticks. Dice the apple. Mix the lemon juice into the vegetables, and then toss with the mayonnaise. Pile into a salad bowl and garnish with the radishes.

AVOCADO, MOZZARELLA AND TOMATO SALAD

An Italian classic, this is a salad of complementary textures and contrasting rich colours. It's important to use ripe, full-flavoured tomatoes. You can serve this as a starter or side salad.

FOR 4

2 ripe avocados, peeled and stone removed	1lb (500g) tomatoes
lemon juice to sprinkle	5 tbs vinaigrette (see page 146)
8 oz (250 g) mozzarella cheese	handful of fresh basil leaves

Slice the avocados and sprinkle immediately with lemon juice to prevent them from going brown. Slice the mozzarella and tomatoes.

Arrange the slices of green avocado, white cheese and red tomato decoratively in a shallow dish. Drizzle the vinaigrette over the top and scatter the basil leaves over the salad just before serving.

OPPOSITE: Carrot Salad (top) and Fennel Salad

134

WATERCRESS SALAD WITH GARLIC CROUTONS ∨

An elegant combination of watercress and crisp lettuce dressed with vinaigrette, this delectable salad has the added treat of crunchy, garlicky croutons.

FOR 4

2 thick slices of bread, crusts removed	2 bunches of watercress
	a handful of crisp lettuce leaves
1 clove garlic, cut in half	
olive oil for frying	6 tbs vinaigrette (see page 146)

Cut the bread into small cubes. Rub the cut side of the garlic over the surface of a frying pan, then discard the garlic. Heat enough oil for shallow frying in the pan, about ½ inch (1 cm), and fry the bread gently until golden brown all over. Remove with a slotted spoon and drain on kitchen paper.

Prepare the watercress and lettuce. Line a salad bowl with the lettuce leaves. Toss the watercress in the vinaigrette until well coated. Pile the watercress inside the lettuce leaves and scatter the croutons over the top.

SPICY RAW MUSHROOM SALAD

Sliced button mushrooms dressed in a slightly curried mayonnaise and sprinkled with fresh coriander make an excellent starter, as well as a tasty addition to a buffet table.

FOR 3–4

12 oz (350 g) small button mushrooms	1 tbs fresh lemon juice
	1 large clove garlic, crushed (optional)
1-2 tsp curry paste	
4 tbs bottled or home-made mayonnaise (see page 150)	fresh coriander leaves to garnish

Slice the mushrooms. Mix the curry paste into the mayonnaise with the lemon juice and add the garlic if desired. Fold in the mushrooms and mix thoroughly until they are well coated in the mayonnaise. Put into a serving dish and garnish with fresh coriander leaves.

Peeling Garlic

Press down on the clove with the flat side of a knife blade, then pull away the burst skin.

OPPOSITE: Watercress Salad with Garlic Croutons

PROVENÇAL PEPPER SALAD ♥

This is a salad redolent of the Mediterranean, with its aromatic fresh herbs and the strong flavours of olives and peppers. Brightly coloured, it makes a lovely lunch dish. Vegans can use potato in place of the eggs.

FOR 6

1 tbs each finely chopped fresh parsley, tarragon, chervil and chives	*2 green peppers*
	6 ripe tomatoes, sliced
1 recipe quantity vinaigrette (see page 146)	*4 hard-boiled eggs, shelled and sliced, or 1 cubed potato, cooked until just tender*
2 red peppers	*24 black olives*

Stir the herbs into the vinaigrette and leave to stand while you prepare the salad.

Skin the red peppers (see page 59) and cut the red and green peppers into long strips. (Green peppers have thinner skin which it is less important to remove.) Place the tomatoes in the bottom of a large, flat serving dish and drizzle one-quarter of the dressing over them. Arrange the pepper strips in a criss-cross pattern on the tomatoes and drizzle with half of the remaining dressing. Cover with the slices of hard-boiled egg and drizzle the rest of the vinaigrette over them. Decorate with olives before serving.

ROASTED PEPPERS WITH MUSHROOMS AND ROCKET ♥

Juicy peppers, tender mushrooms and the earthy flavour of rocket combine to make an original salad. The taste of balsamic vinegar in the garlicky dressing adds a special touch.

FOR 4–6

12 oz (350g) small button mushrooms	*¼ pint (150ml) balsamic garlic and herb dressing (see page 146)*
1 red or yellow pepper, skinned (see page 59) and cut into thick strips	*2 large handfuls of rocket*
2 tbs capers, drained	*8-12 green olives, pitted*

Cut the mushrooms in half, unless they are very tiny. Mix together with the pepper strips and capers, and toss with all but 2 tbs of the dressing. Leave to marinate for 20–30 minutes.

Prepare the rocket and toss with the remaining dressing. Place in the bottom of a salad bowl and arrange the vegetables on top. Garnish with the olives and serve.

OPPOSITE: Provençal Pepper Salad

CAULIFLOWER SALAD WITH MUSTARD MAYONNAISE

A simple salad with a distinctive flavour, this is excellent fare at any time of year, useful for a party or buffet table. It would go well with courgettes with sweetcorn (see page 43) to make a light meal.

FOR 4

2 medium potatoes, peeled and cubed	2 tbs fresh lemon juice
	2 tbs plain set yogurt
1 small cauliflower, cut into florets	1 tbs chopped fresh tarragon
2-3 tsp grainy mustard	2 stalks celery, sliced
3 tbs bottled or home-made mayonnaise (see page 150)	chopped parsley to garnish

Steam the potatoes until just tender. Steam the cauliflower florets for 4–5 minutes or until they are slightly cooked but still crunchy. Cool, and slice them.

Mix the mustard into the mayonnaise, add the lemon juice and stir in the yogurt and the tarragon. Toss the potato, cauliflower and celery gently with this dressing, and put into a dish. Sprinkle with the chopped parsley.

BEETROOT SALAD WITH SOURED CREAM AND GARLIC

A wonderful salad for winter, with rich flavours and beautiful colours – red, pink and green. Cooked beetroot are an excellent addition to many salads; here they play the starring role.

FOR 4

1½ lb (750 g) beetroot, cooked and skinned	3 cloves garlic, crushed
	freshly ground black pepper
¼ pint (150 ml) soured cream	1 tbs chopped fresh parsley or tarragon
1 tbs fresh lemon juice	

Cut the prepared beetroot into medium-thin slices. Mix the soured cream with the lemon juice and garlic and season with pepper. Dress the beetroot, mixing gently until well coated. Pile into a salad bowl and sprinkle with the chopped parsley.

Salads

GREEN BEAN SALAD ꝟ

A salad for summer when green beans come into season, this combination with red onion, dill and garlic is a treat. Capers add an unusual touch.

FOR 4–6

1 lb (500g) French or runner beans, trimmed	*1 small clove garlic, chopped finely*
3 tbs chopped fresh dill or 1½ tbs dried dill	*2 oz (50g) capers*
1 small red onion, diced very small	*sea salt and freshly ground black pepper*
	5 tbs vinaigrette (see page 146)

Steam the prepared beans lightly, so that they are still very crisp. Mix with the dill, onion, garlic and capers, and season lightly with salt and pepper. Dress with the vinaigrette, mix well and serve.

SHREDDED COURGETTE SALAD ꝟ

A fresh and simple salad for late summer, when courgettes are at their best. Fresh ginger, capers and pine nuts add an unusual piquant note. Serve with warm garlic bread.

FOR 6

4 medium courgettes, trimmed	*1 tbs grated fresh ginger*
3 tbs fresh lemon juice	*sea salt and freshly ground black pepper*
2 tbs extra virgin olive oil	
1 medium clove garlic, crushed	*2 tbs capers*
	2 tbs pine nuts

Grate the courgettes and pat them dry with kitchen paper. Combine the lemon juice, olive oil, garlic, ginger, salt and pepper in a small jar and shake to blend. Pour the dressing over the courgettes and add the capers and pine nuts. Mix thoroughly and serve immediately. (If left to stand it will go watery.)

TECHNICOLOR BEAN SALAD ❣

A bright salad with interesting flavours, this is tossed in a very garlicky vinaigrette. It makes an excellent addition to a buffet table, or it can be served as a starter or part of a light meal.

FOR 6

2 x 14oz (400g) cans mixed beans (or equivalent cooked dried beans such as haricot, black-eyed, red kidney etc, see page 185)	*For the garlic dressing:*
	juice of ½ lemon
	2-3 tbs wine vinegar
	1 tsp sea salt
8oz (250g) French beans, trimmed	*4 large cloves garlic, chopped finely*
6-8 spring onions, chopped finely	*freshly ground black pepper*
medium bunch of parsley, chopped finely	*¼ pint (150ml) extra virgin olive oil*

To make the dressing, mix together the lemon juice, vinegar, salt and garlic in a bowl and add lots of freshly ground black pepper. Stirring all the time, dribble in the olive oil so that the dressing thickens as you work it. Check the seasoning.

Drain the canned beans and rinse them. Drain thoroughly. Steam the French beans for 5–6 minutes or until just tender. Toss all the beans together with the spring onions, then add the garlic dressing and toss again. Sprinkle the chopped parsley over the top. Serve at room temperature.

PASTA AND BEAN SALAD WITH BASIL AND PECORINO

An alluring mixture of peppers, green beans and kidney beans, pasta and herbs, this salad's finishing touch is finely pared cheese. It's really a meal in itself, served with warm fresh bread.

FOR 6

8oz (250g) pasta bows	*3 tbs chopped parsley*
1 red pepper, skinned (see page 59) and cut into thin slices	*¼ pint (150ml) soy and lemon dressing (see page 147)*
1 yellow pepper, skinned (see page 59) and cut into thin slices	*handful of fresh basil leaves, shredded*
6oz (175g) green beans, cooked	*2oz (50g) pecorino cheese, pared finely into shavings*
4oz (125g) kidney beans (canned or cooked dried, see page 185)	

Cook the pasta bows in boiling water until 'al dente' (see page 90). Drain, and rinse immediately under cold water in the colander.

Mix the peppers, pasta bows, green beans, kidney beans and parsley in a salad bowl, add the dressing and toss until thoroughly mixed together. Finally, fold in the basil and garnish with the pecorino shavings.

OPPOSITE: Technicolor Bean Salad with its dressing

CURRIED PASTA SALAD ♥

A main-dish salad with plenty of bite and zest. You can add chopped mango for an exotic touch, plus a garnish of fresh coriander leaves if you like.

FOR 4

12oz (350g) pasta shells	For the dressing:
1 tsp extra virgin olive oil	¼ pint (150ml) extra virgin olive oil
8oz (250g) baby mushrooms	
3 spring onions, chopped	4 tbs white wine vinegar
2 stalks celery, sliced thinly	2 tbs fresh lemon juice
	2 tbs light soft brown sugar
	1½ tbs curry powder

Cook the pasta until 'al dente' (see page 90), then drain thoroughly and rinse under cold water. Toss thoroughly with the oil, mixing with your hands so that the pasta shells are separated. Add the mushrooms, spring onions and celery.

Mix together the dressing ingredients, add to the pasta salad and toss well. Refrigerate for 1 hour or overnight, but serve at room temperature.

ORANGE RICE SALAD ♥

The unusual method of cooking rice in orange juice gives it an exceptional flavour. A tasty mixture of pimientos and mangetout, plus some red onion, is added to the rice to make up an unusual and delectable salad.

FOR 6

6oz (175g) long-grain rice	4oz (125g) mangetout, trimmed and sliced
1 pint (600 ml) fresh orange juice	
2 canned pimientos, drained and cut into strips	2 large oranges, peeled and divided into segments
1 small red onion, chopped finely	7-8 tbs vinaigrette (see page 146)

Rinse the rice and put into a saucepan with the orange juice. Bring to the boil. Stir once, then cover tightly and cook very gently for 15 minutes or until the liquid is absorbed and the rice tender. Fluff it up with a fork and leave to cool in a bowl.

Mix the prepared vegetables into the cooled rice. Cut up the orange segments and mix them in. Toss thoroughly with the vinaigrette, and it is ready to serve.

SALAD DRESSINGS

S alad dressings can be made with a wide variety of oils and vinegars, plus flavourings such as garlic, fresh herbs, fresh ginger and mustard. In some cases, you don't need to make the dressing beforehand, mixing it in a bowl or jar – just combine the ingredients in the bottom of the salad bowl, then add the salad and toss together.

Oils for salad dressings include:

• corn oil, which is odourless and very bland. It is high in polyunsaturates.

• groundnut oil, pressed from peanuts, which is clear and mild in flavour; the Chinese version has a distinctive taste of peanuts. Groundnut oil is about 50 per cent monounsaturated fat and 30 per cent polyunsaturated.

• olive oil, which has a distinctive fruity flavour. Unrefined extra virgin oil is obtained from a first cold pressing of the olives; it has a stronger flavour and greener colour than other olive oils, and is preferred for dressings. It is high in monounsaturated fat.

• sesame oil, expressed from sesame seeds, which gives an oriental flavouring. Light-coloured sesame oil has a delicious nutty flavour; the darker oils are too strong for salad dressings. Sesame oil is high in polyunsaturates.

• sunflower oil, which has a delicate flavour and pale yellow colour. It is very high in polyunsaturates.

• walnut oil, which has a nutty taste and fragrance.

Other nuts pressed for oil include hazelnut and almond. Use these rich, strongly flavoured oils sparingly, mixing them with a blander oil.

Vinegars to choose from include:

• cider, which has a clean, sharp, fruity taste. It is said to have health-giving properties.

• balsamic, a very fine vinegar from Italy, which is made from fermented grapes and aged in wood barrels. It is dark brown, thick, aromatic and full-flavoured, so is normally used in moderation.

• raspberry and other fruit vinegars, which are increasingly popular. They give a full fruity flavour and rich colour.

• red wine, which is similar in flavour to white wine vinegar, but slightly mellower. It gives a denser, darker quality to a salad dressing.

• sherry, which has a distinctive flavour and aroma. It gives an unusual quality to dressings.

• white wine, one of the most commonly used. It gives a pungent tang to dressings. White wine vinegar is often infused with herbs, such as tarragon, rosemary, sage and mint, as well as garlic or mixed herbs with chilli.

The best herbs to use for salad dressings are basil, chives, coriander, dill, fennel, marjoram, parsley and thyme. For the maximum flavour, infuse the freshly chopped herb in the dressing for up to half an hour before using.

VINAIGRETTE ᴠ

*H*ere's a recipe for the basic dressing that can be used for almost any salad. Experiment with different oils, vinegars and mustards, to find the combination you like best, and vary the ingredients to suit the salads too.

FOR 4–6

1-2 tsp mild or grainy mustard	sea salt and freshly ground black pepper
2 tbs fresh lemon juice	5 tbs extra virgin olive oil
2 tbs wine vinegar, balsamic vinegar or cider vinegar	crushed garlic to taste (optional)

Mix the mustard with the lemon juice and vinegar and season with salt and pepper. Stir in the olive oil gradually so that the dressing thickens as you work. It should become creamy in consistency. Stir in the garlic (if using). Allow to stand for up to 30 minutes before using, to allow the flavours to develop.

BALSAMIC GARLIC AND HERB DRESSING ᴠ

MAKES 4 fl oz (125 ml)

3-4 tbs balsamic vinegar	1 tbs chopped parsley
2 cloves garlic, crushed	1 tsp chopped fresh tarragon,
sea salt and freshly ground black pepper	basil or any combination of favourite herb
5 tbs extra virgin olive oil	

Mix the balsamic vinegar with the garlic and seasoning to taste. Gradually add the olive oil, whisking all the time so that the dressing amalgamates. Whisk in the herbs.

GARLIC MUSTARD DRESSING ᴠ

MAKES about 14 fl oz (400 ml)

juice of ½ lemon	6 cloves garlic, crushed
3-4 tbs mild mustard	½ pint (300 ml) extra virgin olive oil
4 tbs red wine vinegar	
sea salt and freshly ground black pepper	

Put the lemon juice, mustard and vinegar into the blender and season with salt and pepper. Blend until well mixed, then add the garlic. Start adding the olive oil in a dribble, gradually increasing to a slow steady stream. When all the oil has been incorporated check the seasoning. Store in an airtight container in the fridge.

You can also make this without a blender: stir vigorously with a whisk as you slowly add the oil in a thin stream.

POPPY SEED DRESSING ᴠ

MAKES 1 pint (600 ml)

2 oz (50g) caster sugar or honey	3 tbs grated sweet onion
1 tbs mild mustard	14 fl oz (400 ml) extra virgin olive oil
4 tbs red wine vinegar	3 tbs poppy seeds
sea salt	2 tbs fresh lemon juice

Combine the sugar or honey, mustard, vinegar, salt to taste and grated onion in a food processor and run the machine for 1 minute. Then pour in the oil in a slow steady stream with the machine running. When all the oil has been incorporated, check the seasoning. Stir in the poppy seeds and lemon juice. Keep refrigerated until ready to use.

SOY AND LEMON DRESSING v

MAKES ¼ pint (150 ml)

juice of 1 lemon	*1 tsp grated fresh ginger*
3-4 tbs soy sauce	*1 clove garlic, crushed*
6 tbs dark sesame oil	*freshly ground black pepper*

Mix all the ingredients together in a small bowl until well blended.

THOUSAND ISLAND DRESSING

MAKES about ½ pint (300 ml)

½ pint (300 ml) bottled or home-made mayonnaise (see page 150)	*2 tbs finely chopped dill-pickled cucumber (optional)*
4 tbs tomato ketchup	*2 tbs fresh lemon juice*
2 tbs finely chopped parsley (optional)	

Mix all the ingredients together and keep refrigerated until ready to use.

LEMONY CAPER VINAIGRETTE v

MAKES about ½ pint (300 ml)

¼ pint (150 ml) extra virgin olive oil	*snipped fresh chives (optional)*
4 fl oz (125 ml) fresh lemon juice	*finely chopped shallots (optional)*
1 tbs capers, chopped	*sea salt and freshly ground black pepper*
1-2 tbs mild mustard (optional)	

Combine all the ingredients in a screw-top jar and shake until well blended.

YOGURT DRESSING

FOR 4-6

6 tbs plain yogurt	*finely chopped green or red pepper (optional)*
2 tbs fresh lemon juice	*sea salt and freshly ground black pepper*
1 tbs grated mild onion	
1 tbs celery seed	
crushed garlic to taste	

Mix all the ingredients together and season to taste.

BLUE CHEESE DRESSING

MAKES about 7 fl oz (200 ml)

1-2 tsp mild or grainy mustard	*2 oz (50g) Danish blue cheese or any favourite blue cheese, crumbled*
3 tbs fresh lemon juice	*4 fl oz (125 ml) extra virgin olive oil*
2 tbs wine vinegar	*freshly ground black pepper*

Mix the mustard with the lemon juice and vinegar. Add the crumbled cheese and mash thoroughly. Gradually add the olive oil, stirring until the dressing is completely smooth. Season to taste with lots of pepper.

Flower garnishes

Many common flowers, both garden and wild, are edible. They make great additions to salads, or can be used as stuffing garnishes. When your herbs flower in spring and early summer add the flowers to your salads along with the chopped leaves. Lovely scented rose petals can be used as the summer progresses.

You can also choose from the following:

allium, apple blossoms, carnations and pinks, courgette, cornflowers, daisies, geraniums, gladioli, hawthorn, honeysuckle, hop flowers, hibiscus, jasmine, lavender, lilac, lime flowers, mallow, marigolds, nasturtiums, pansies, pea flowers, plum blossoms, radish flower, rosemary, snapdragons, stocks, strawberry flowers and violets.

CHAPTER EIGHT

Sauces and Dips

In many of the great cuisines of the world there are traditional sauces made purely with vegetables and dairy products. Hollandaise and mayonnaise are two well-known examples from classic French cooking; pesto from Italy and salsa from Mexico are two more that have caught the global imagination in recent years. Sweet and sour sauce from the East has long been widely loved, as has American barbecue sauce.

A good sauce will enhance the delicate flavours of meatless dishes, and adds elegance and interest to home-cooked meals. The recipes in this section are just a small sample of the enormous worldwide repertoire of sauces – sauces for pasta, sauces to go with meatless meatballs or loaf, sauces for pastry dishes, sauces for potatoes and other plainly cooked vegetables, and thicker sauces to be served as dips for raw vegetables, fruit, bread and tortilla chips.

ROASTED RED PEPPER SAUCE

This sauce needs no seasoning – it has an absolutely amazing flavour, which comes from roasting the peppers, and the most beautiful colour.

MAKES ¹/₂ pint (300 ml)

2 large red peppers	2 tbs flour
¹/₂ pint (300 ml) vegetable stock	2-3 tbs crème fraîche or single
1 oz (25g) margarine	cream

Cut the peppers in half and deseed them. Place on a baking tray and roast at 200°C/400°F/gas 6 for 15–20 minutes, then cool. Skin them, chop roughly and blend with the stock to a thin purée.

Heat the margarine, stir in the flour and gradually stir in the purée with a wooden spoon. When it is thickened and smooth, simmer gently for 3–4 minutes. Remove from the heat, stir in the crème fraîche or single cream and serve.

TARRAGON AND MUSTARD SAUCE

A fine sauce that turns the simplest of meals into something special. Try it with the vegetable terrine on page 81, stuffed peppers (page 68) or cottage crunch casserole (page 67).

MAKES ¹/₂ pint (300 ml)

1 oz (25g) margarine	1 tbs cornflour
4 tbs chopped fresh tarragon or 2 tbs dried tarragon	4 fl oz (125 ml) milk
1 tbs mild mustard	¹/₄ pint (150 ml) crème fraîche or single cream

Melt the margarine and cook the tarragon in it very gently for 2–3 minutes. Stir in the mustard and mix well. Sprinkle in the cornflour and stir until smooth, then gradually add the milk, stirring all the time. When the sauce is smooth and thick, stir in the crème fraîche. The sauce needs no further seasoning – the tarragon flavour does it all.

SIMPLE PESTO SAUCE ▾

This version of pesto has no cheese or nuts in it, and it is simple, fresh and irresistible. Serve with fresh pasta for a quick, delicious meal.

MAKES 2 fl oz (60 ml)

8-10 large cloves garlic, crushed or chopped	4 tbs olive oil
2 large bunches fresh basil, chopped	

Combine the ingredients in a bowl and mix together. Chill before using.

For traditional pesto, add 4 tbs pine nuts and 3 oz (75 g) freshly grated Parmesan cheese. Pound all the ingredients together in a mortar and pestle, or blend until creamy in a blender or food processor. Store in an airtight jar in the refrigerator.

HOLLANDAISE

An elegant sauce for steamed vegetables through the seasons, either hot or cold. It is also delicious with crudités as a starter. If you like, stir in a little Greek yogurt or crème fraîche.

FOR 4

3 tbs white wine vinegar	*fresh lemon juice to taste*
2 tbs cold water	*sea salt and freshly ground*
3 free-range egg yolks, beaten	*black pepper*
6oz (175g) margarine, warmed	

Boil the vinegar and water hard until reduced to 1 tbs. Put into a bowl and place it over gently heating water in a saucepan. Add the egg yolks and stir thoroughly, then gradually stir in little portions of the margarine. Stir constantly. If the sauce thickens too quickly add a few drops of cold water. Do not overheat. Season to taste with lemon juice, salt and pepper.

MAYONNAISE

The homemade version of this most popular of sauces is far superior to any bought one. Resist any temptation to add the oil faster than the recipe describes: it will not emulsify (thicken) well if you do.

MAKES ½ pint (300 ml)

1 free-range egg	*sea salt and freshly ground*
1 tsp Dijon mustard	*black pepper*
½ pint (300ml) olive or sunflower oil	*fresh lemon juice to taste*

Break the egg into the bowl of the blender and add the mustard. Blend until well mixed, then start to add the oil drop by drop, with the machine running. After a while increase to a thin stream; as the mayonnaise thickens you can increase the flow of oil even more. When all the oil has been added, continue to blend for another minute to thicken up the mayonnaise. Season to taste with salt, pepper and lemon juice.

GREEN HERB MAYONNAISE

MAKES ½ pint (300 ml)

2 tbs chopped fresh tarragon or dill	*2 tbs chopped baby spinach leaves*
2 tbs each chopped parsley, chives and watercress	*½ pint (300ml) mayonnaise (see left)*

Chop the herbs and leaves finely in a food processor. Add them to the mayonnaise and stir in thoroughly.

The Food Processor

If you haven't already got one, a food processor is the best investment you can make as a keen cook. It does so many things, and much faster than you can do them yourself. It makes wonderful smooth soups; it shreds vegetables in an instant; it makes vegetable purées without effort; it grates, slices and chops very very finely; it makes breadcrumbs and pastry dough; and it will produce worry-free mayonnaise and other emulsion sauces.

RICH TOMATO SAUCE ⌄

This goes really well with pasta, as well as with the beanburgers on page 55, anything grilled on the barbecue, and with toad in the hole (see page 63).

FOR 6

3½ lb (1.5 kg) ripe tomatoes, skinned (see page 59), or 2 x 1½ lb (700g) cans tomatoes, drained	6 oz (175g) tomato purée
	1 tbs chopped fresh oregano or tarragon
2 tbs olive oil	1 tbs each chopped fresh basil and thyme
1 large onion, chopped	sea salt and freshly ground pepper
2 tbs chopped garlic	

Cut fresh or canned tomatoes into small cubes. Heat the olive oil and sauté the onion and garlic, stirring, for 1 minute. Add the chopped tomatoes and the tomato purée, then the herbs. Stir well and bring to a simmer. Cook over a very low heat, covered, for 20–25 minutes. Season to taste.

LIGHT TOMATO SAUCE ⌄

The simplest possible way of making tomato sauce, and beautifully healthy. Use plum tomatoes when they are in season; at other times of the year, make the sauce with canned tomatoes.

FOR 2–3

1 x 14 oz (400g) can tomatoes, or same weight fresh tomatoes, skinned (see page 59) and chopped	1 tbs dried mixed herbs
	1 large clove garlic, crushed
2 shallots or 4 spring onions, chopped finely	sea salt and freshly ground black pepper

Put all the ingredients into the blender and blend until smooth. Season to taste. Heat through gently for 5–6 minutes before serving.

BELOW: (left to right) Hollandaise, Simple Pesto, Rich Tomato and Light Tomato sauces

NO-COOK SALSA ❤

So quick and easy to make, this fresh sauce gives the taste buds some vigorous exercise and is indispensable with Mexican food (see pages 33 to 39).

FOR 2–3

4 large tomatoes, skinned (see page 59) and chopped (canned or fresh)	1 fresh chilli, sliced
	small bunch of fresh coriander, chopped
2 spring onions, chopped	

Put the ingredients into the blender and work until smooth. Store in an airtight jar in the refrigerator.

TOMATO AND CHILLI SALSA ❤

An easy, quickly made sauce, this is lovely with barbecued foods (see pages 119 to 125), and with anything Mexican (see pages 33 to 39).

FOR 2–3

5 tomatoes, skinned (see page 59) and cubed small	½ purple or red onion, chopped finely
juice of 1½ lemons	sea salt
6oz (175g) canned mild green chillies, chopped small, or fresh chillies to taste	1 tbs chopped fresh coriander (optional)

Mix all the ingredients together and simmer for 10–15 minutes over a very gentle heat. Season to taste with a little salt and stir in the optional coriander.

CHILLI SAUCE ❤

A full-blooded chilli sauce, rich and full of flavour. It is always welcome at a barbecue party. Try it with the quesadillas on page 33 as well as the meatless meatballs (see page 73) or loaf (page 62).

MAKES ¾ pint (450 ml)

1 sweet onion, chopped small	1 x 14oz (400g) can chopped tomatoes with juice, or same weight fresh tomatoes, skinned (see page 59) and chopped
1 tbs olive oil	
1 large clove garlic, crushed	
1-2 fresh green chillies, sliced finely	juice of ½ lemon
	sea salt

Soften the onion in the olive oil over a low heat, covered with a lid, for 5–6 minutes. Add the garlic and chilli and cook for a few minutes longer, until the chilli is well softened. Add the tomatoes and heat through for 5 minutes. Finish with the lemon juice and season to taste with salt. Keep refrigerated in an airtight jar.

> ### *Chilli Heat*
> If using fresh chillies, remove the seeds and veins first if you want to control the heat.

BARBECUE SAUCE v

The perfect sauce for marinating vegetables before you put them on the barbecue – sharp, and full of flavour. Hand it around to go with barbecued vegetables as well as vegetarian burgers and sausages.

MAKES 1 pint (600 ml)

12 oz (350g) tomato ketchup	*2 heaped tbs soft brown sugar*
juice of 1 lemon	*2 tbs olive oil*
¼ pint (150 ml) red or white wine vinegar	*2 tbs mild mustard*
	2 tbs sweet cucumber relish
6 cloves garlic, crushed	

Put the tomato ketchup into a bowl with the lemon juice. Measure the vinegar and pour it into the ketchup bottle; shake well so that you clean the bottle, and add the liquid to the bowl. Mix thoroughly, then stir in the rest of the ingredients and it is ready to use. Keep refrigerated in an airtight jar.

SWEET AND SOUR SAUCE v

A classic sauce to go with Chinese egg fried rice (see page 94) or with steamed or grilled vegetables. You can also toss it into stir-fried vegetables just before serving, and it's indispensable at a barbecue!

MAKES ½ pint (300 ml)

¼ pint (150 ml) pineapple juice	*1 inch (2.5 cm) root ginger, peeled and grated finely*
3 tbs olive oil	*2 cloves garlic, crushed*
3 tbs light soft brown sugar	*4 tbs fresh lemon juice*
1 tbs soy sauce or more to taste	*1 heaped tbs cornflour*
	freshly ground black pepper

Combine the pineapple juice, oil, sugar, soy sauce, ginger, garlic and 2 tbs of the lemon juice in a saucepan. Heat until the sugar dissolves. Mix the cornflour with the remaining lemon juice, add to the pan and stir until the sauce is smooth and thick. Season with pepper. Simmer very gently for 5 minutes, stirring occasionally.

MIXED WILD MUSHROOM SAUCE

The exquisite flavours of wild or Chinese mushrooms in this light, creamy sauce makes it the perfect sauce for pasta. You can also serve it with the rice and vegetable cheese bake on page 100, the mille-feuilles with baby vegetables (page 116) or meatless meatballs (page 73).

FOR 3–4

12 oz (350g) wild or Chinese mushrooms, e.g. ceps, chanterelles, field mushrooms, shiitake, oyster etc

2 tbs olive oil

sea salt and freshly ground black pepper

2 tbs chopped fresh thyme or 1 tbs dried thyme

½ pint (300ml) crème fraîche or single cream

2 tbs fresh lemon juice

Slice the mushrooms into even lengths. Sauté them in the olive oil until the juices run a little; don't let the mushrooms go too soft. Season to taste with salt and pepper. Add the thyme and stir in. Slowly add the crème fraîche or cream and heat through for 3–4 minutes. Add the lemon juice and check the seasoning.

MEATLESS BOLOGNESE SAUCE ❧

This famous sauce is easy and always popular. You can flavour it as you like by adding extra herbs, garlic or spices to suit the family's tastes. It freezes well and is a useful standby to have on hand.

FOR 4

1 large onion, sliced

2-3 large cloves garlic, sliced finely

2 tbs olive oil

4 oz (125g) mushrooms, sliced

8 oz (250g) vegetarian mince

2 x 14 oz (400g) cans chopped tomatoes, with juice

1 tbs each chopped fresh parsley and chives

¼-½ tsp cayenne pepper (optional)

sea salt and freshly ground black pepper

Cook the onion and garlic in the oil over a gentle heat, covered with a lid, for 10 minutes or until quite soft. Stir occasionally. Stir in the mushrooms and vegetarian mince and cook, stirring, for 5 minutes. Then add the tomatoes and herbs and simmer for 5–6 minutes or until well amalgamated. Season to taste with cayenne, salt and black pepper.

BÉCHAMEL SAUCE

MAKES ¾ pint (450 ml)

2 oz (50 g) butter or margarine	pinch of grated nutmeg
3 tbs plain flour	sea salt and freshly ground pepper
¾ pint (450 ml) skimmed or soya milk, warmed	

Melt the butter in a small, heavy-bottomed saucepan. Gradually stir in the flour, using a wooden spoon. Add the warm milk slowly, stirring all the time until the sauce thickens. Season to taste with nutmeg, salt and pepper and simmer over a very low heat for 5–6 minutes.

For ½ pint (300 ml) béchamel, use 1½ oz (40 g) butter or margarine, 2 tbs plain flour and ½ pint (300 ml) milk.

CHEESE AND PARSLEY SAUCE

*T*his popular sauce goes wonderfully well with the cottage crunch casserole on page 67. Its flavours also complement pasties (see page 112), meatless loaf (page 62) and the savoury vegetable strudel on page 110.

MAKES ¾ pint (450 ml)

1½ oz (40 g) margarine	medium bunch of parsley, chopped finely
2 tbs plain flour	
1 tbs mild mustard	¼ pint (150 ml) crème fraîche or single cream (or more milk)
¼ pint (150 ml) skimmed or soya milk	
	freshly ground black pepper
2 oz (50 g) Cheddar cheese, grated	

Melt the margarine in a heavy-bottomed saucepan and stir in the flour. When well mixed, stir in the mustard. Slowly add the milk, stirring all the time so that the sauce becomes smooth and thick. Add the grated cheese and the parsley and cook gently for 5 minutes. Add the cream or extra milk, stir until completely smooth, and season to taste with black pepper.

GRAVY ⱱ

A standby for so many meals, this gravy is wonderful with the meatless meatballs on page 73, the meatless loaf (page 62), with vegetarian sausages and, of course, dumplings (see page 31).

MAKES 1 pint (600 ml)

1 onion, chopped small	1-2 tbs soy sauce or tomato purée
1½ oz (40 g) margarine	
4 oz (125 g) mushrooms, chopped small	sea salt and freshly ground black pepper
3-4 tbs gravy granules	
1 pint (600 ml) boiling water or stock	

Soften the onion in the margarine for 4–5 minutes over a low heat, covered with a lid. Add the mushrooms and cook until the juices run. Add the gravy granules to the boiling water and stir until thick. Pour on to the vegetables and stir until well amalgamated. Season to taste with soy sauce or tomato purée, and add salt and pepper if necessary.

SPICY CHILLI DIP v

*I*f you like the heat of chilli, this dip is for you – and it's quite substantial, too, being made with beans. Lovely with corn chips, pitta bread, raw mushrooms and a selection of crudités.

FOR 4

6oz (175g) canned tomatoes	*3 spring onions, sliced*
6oz (175g) canned kidney beans	*1 fresh red chilli, sliced*
1 tbs tomato purée	*sea salt and freshly ground black pepper*
dash of soy sauce	*chopped fresh coriander to garnish*
2 large cloves garlic, crushed	
½ red pepper, deseeded and chopped	

Put all the prepared ingredients into the blender and blend until smooth. Season to taste, and serve garnished with chopped coriander.

DILL CUCUMBER DIP

*T*his pale green dip has a lovely summery flavour, and makes light food for hot weather. Serve with crisps, raw vegetables or granary toast, or as a sauce for a main dish.

FOR 4

½ cucumber, grated	*1 tbs finely chopped onion*
½ pint (300ml) soured cream	*juice of ½ lemon*
4 tbs chopped fresh dill	*sea salt and freshly ground black pepper*
2 tbs dried dillweed	

Squeeze the grated cucumber dry then pat on kitchen paper. Put all the ingredients into a bowl and mix thoroughly. Put into a dish and chill for at least 1 hour before serving.

AMERICAN SOURED CREAM DIP

*S*implicity itself, this dip is amazingly delicious and a huge favourite. Serve with tortilla chips, crisps and a selection of crudités.

FOR 4–6

1 packet dried onion soup mix (approx 2oz/50g)	*¾ pint (450ml) soured cream*

Stir the dried soup into the soured cream and put into a decorative bowl. Chill for 1 hour or so before serving.

REFRIED BEAN DIP

*T*he satisfying flavours and textures of this dip, inspired by Mexican cookery, make it a firm favourite at parties. Taco sauces are widely available in supermarkets and make a useful standby on the larder shelf. Serve the dip alongside tortilla chips with drinks before a meal, at any time of the year.

FOR 4–6

8oz (250g) canned refried beans	*4-5 spring onions, sliced finely*
2-3 tbs taco sauce	*1-2 tsp chilli relish*
4oz (125g) Cheddar cheese, grated	*8 fl oz (250ml) crème fraîche or soured cream*
	sea salt

Heat the refried beans gently, mashing them with the taco sauce. Stir in the cheese until it melts, then add the spring onions and chilli relish to taste. Stir in the crème fraîche or soured cream and heat through. Season with salt, and serve warm or cold.

ARTICHOKE DIP

A delicately flavoured dip that goes very well on a mixed buffet table. Or hand it around with corn chips or raw vegetables, as a nibble before a meal.

FOR 4

8oz (250g) artichoke hearts, canned or freshly cooked	*2oz (50g) pecorino cheese, grated*
½ red onion, chopped finely	*¼ pint (150ml) mayonnaise (see page 150)*
1 clove garlic, crushed	
2 tbs finely chopped parsley	*sea salt and freshly ground black pepper*
1 tbs chopped fresh oregano or 1 tsp dried oregano	

Put all the ingredients into the blender and blend until smooth. Season to taste and chill. Serve with corn chips, sliced carrots or celery.

GUACAMOLE ♥

T here are endless versions of this famous Mexican avocado dip: here is mine! Serve with tortilla chips, pitta bread, or raw mushrooms, celery, carrots and other crudités of your choice.

FOR 4–6

2 tomatoes, skinned (see page 59) and chopped	*2 cloves garlic, sliced finely (optional)*
juice of 2 large lemons	*4 spring onions, sliced finely (optional)*
1 small fresh red chilli, sliced very finely, or 1 x 4oz (125g) can mild green chillies, chopped finely	*2 large avocados, mashed*
	sea salt and freshly ground black pepper

Combine all the ingredients except the avocado in the food processor and work until very smooth. Stir in the avocado with a fork and season to taste. Put into a decorative bowl.

GREEN HERB DIP

S uperb for a summer party, fresh, aromatic herbs give their wonderful qualities to this creamy green dip. Serve it with raw vegetables to scoop it up, tortilla chips and strips of pitta bread. It also makes a delicious sauce for pasta.

FOR 6–8

3 tbs chopped parsley	*½ pint (300ml) mayonnaise (see page 150)*
3 tbs chopped fresh dill	
bunch of watercress, chopped	*½ pint (300ml) soured cream*
3 spring onions, sliced finely	*sea salt and freshly ground black pepper*
6oz (175g) cooked, drained spinach, squeezed dry	*small pinch of paprika*

Put the chopped parsley, dill and watercress into the food processor and blend until they are chopped very finely. Turn into a bowl and add the spring onions. Blend the cooked spinach until very smooth. Add to the herbs and stir in the mayonnaise. Mix thoroughly, then stir in the soured cream. Season to taste with salt, pepper and paprika and chill before serving.

CHAPTER NINE

Desserts, Cakes and Biscuits

Very few people can resist a really delicious dessert or slice of cake, even when they think they should. But judicious amounts of something sweet at regular intervals are not such a bad thing for general health!

The irresistible appeal of a tiramisù or a pecan pie is undeniable, and desserts like this can grace the table at any time of the year. Crème brûlée, sticky toffee pudding and luscious chocolate desserts are everybody's favourites, ideal for all seasons. Fruit desserts are well-loved, too. Fruit salads and sorbets make good use of fragrant soft fruits in summer, but autumn is the time when fruits really come into their own, with crisp apples, blackberries and blueberries as well as fresh nuts. You can freeze some of this produce – apples in the form of a purée, or berries just as they are. Then, in the chill depths of winter or early spring, you can still produce an exquisite pie, tart or cheesecake.

Classic cakes – lemon, chocolate, carrot and mixed fruit – and biscuits are also a part of the pleasures of home cooking and family life.

CHOCOLATE MOUSSE

A divinely rich dessert that shows why chocolate mousse is such a universal favourite! For the best flavour, use a good-quality dark dessert chocolate.

FOR 4–6

4 oz (125g) plain chocolate, broken into small pieces	*8 fl oz (250ml) double cream or crème fraîche*
3 size-1 free-range eggs, separated	*3 tbsp caster sugar*
1½ tbs water	*whipped cream and grated chocolate to decorate*
2 tbs sweet liqueur such as Chartreuse, Amaretto or Grand Marnier	

Put the chocolate in a small heatproof bowl and set in a pan of hot water to melt. Alternatively, melt in the microwave. Set aside to cool slightly.

Combine the egg yolks and water in a large heatproof bowl and set over a pan of simmering water. Whisk for a minute or so until the yolks start to thicken, being extremely careful not to let them curdle. Add the liqueur and continue whisking until the mixture is pale, very thick and increased in volume. Remove from the heat.

Add the melted chocolate to the whisked mixture and fold it in gently but thoroughly.

Whip the cream or crème fraîche until it starts to thicken. Add 1 tbs of the sugar and continue whipping until thick. Fold into the chocolate mixture.

In a clean bowl, whisk the egg whites until soft peaks will form. Add the remaining sugar and continue whisking until stiff. Fold the egg whites into the chocolate mixture.

Spoon the mousse into a serving bowl or individual ramekins. Cover and chill. When ready to serve, decorate with whipped cream and grated chocolate.

FROZEN VANILLA MOUSSE

T his mousse is like a simple ice cream made without a custard. The mousse can also be made with Greek yogurt, rather than cream, and sweetened with honey instead of sugar. You can stir a little stewed fresh or dried fruit or chopped nuts into the cream mixture before folding in the egg white, to vary the flavour.

FOR 3–4

8 fl oz (250ml) whipping cream	*1 free-range egg white*
1 oz (25g) icing sugar, sifted	*¼ tsp salt*
½ tsp vanilla essence	

Whip the cream until it is starting to thicken. Add the icing sugar and vanilla and continue whipping until the cream is thick.

In another bowl, whisk the egg white with the salt until stiff. Fold the egg white into the cream mixture. Spoon into a mould or ice cube tray, cover and freeze without stirring. Serve with a sauce or with crushed soft fruits.

RASPBERRY MOUSSE

This basic fruit mousse can be endlessly varied, using other fruits (in season or frozen) with their matching jelly or a contrasting flavour. Vegetarian jellies use agar agar, made from seaweed, as the setting agent, rather than gelatine (which is derived from animals).

FOR 4

3oz (85g) vegetarian raspberry jelly crystals

1 pint (600ml) water

½ pint (300ml) whipping cream

8oz (250g) fresh or thawed frozen raspberries

whipped cream and chopped nuts to decorate

Make the jelly with the water as directed on the packet. Leave it to cool but not set.

Whip the cream. Whip the jelly and fold in the whipped cream. Fold in the fruit. Pour into a dish or mould and chill until set.

Serve in the dish, or turned out of the mould, decorated with whipped cream and chopped nuts.

Since vegetarian jelly sets less hard than regular jelly, some separation may occur. If this happens, mix the mousse up again and serve in the dish, decorated as above.

FRUIT SORBET ᵥ

A refreshing fruit sorbet is the perfect dessert in hot weather. You can make it sweet or a little tart, according to your taste. If you don't have an ice-cream machine, you can freeze the sorbet in an ice cube tray, whisking it two or three times to break up ice crystals.

FOR 6

1½lb (750g) fresh or frozen raspberries, strawberries or other fruit of your choice

about 4oz (125g) sugar

4 tbs water

juice of 1 lemon

Purée the fruit in a blender or food processor. If it has small pips (as raspberries do), press the purée through a sieve.

Combine the sugar and water in a saucepan and heat, stirring to dissolve the sugar. Bring to the boil and boil the syrup until it reaches 113°C/230°F on a sugar thermometer. Remove from the heat and leave to cool.

When the syrup is cold, mix it with the fruit purée and stir in the lemon juice. Taste the mixture and add more sugar or lemon juice if liked: the flavour should be quite strong.

Pour into an ice-cream machine and freeze until firm.

OPPOSITE: Raspberry Mousse (large dish) and Raspberry Sorbet

BAKED CHOCOLATE PUDDING WITH FUDGE SAUCE

*W*ho can resist this combination, the chocolate cake smelling so good in the oven and served warm, soaked in fudge sauce. A real family favourite.

FOR 6

6oz (175g) margarine	*1 tsp vanilla essence*
6oz (175g) light soft brown sugar	
6oz (175g) plain flour	*For the fudge sauce:*
2oz (50g) wholemeal flour	*6oz (175g) light soft brown sugar*
2oz (50g) cocoa powder	
3 tsp baking powder	*7 fl oz (200ml) single cream*
4 free-range eggs, beaten	*1oz (25g) margarine*

Cream the margarine with the sugar until light and fluffy. Sift the flours with the cocoa and baking powder (tip the bran from the sieve into the mixture). Beat the flour mixture into the creamed mixture alternately with the eggs, beating until light. Add the vanilla. Turn into an 8 inch (20 cm) round ovenproof dish and bake at 190°C/375°F/gas 5 for 40–45 minutes or until a sharp knife inserted in the centre comes out clean.

Meanwhile, make the sauce: put the sugar, cream and margarine into a heavy-bottomed saucepan. Bring to the boil, stirring to dissolve the sugar, and then turn the heat down until the mixture is simmering. Cook for about 5 minutes or until it is thick.

Pour the sauce over the hot pudding and leave to stand for up to an hour or so before eating, so that the cake has a chance to soak up the sauce.

TIRAMISÙ

*T*his is an absolutely brilliant version of a world-famous dessert – slightly less rich than some recipes, but full of that coffee flavour, and well laced with brandy!

FOR 4–6

¼ pint (150ml) strong black coffee	*4oz (125g) plain yogurt*
2 tbs brandy	*4oz (125g) ricotta cheese*
6oz (175g) sponge fingers (boudoir biscuits)	*4oz (125g) caster sugar*
	1 tsp vanilla essence
8oz (250g) mascarpone or full fat soft cheese	*3 free-range egg whites*
	1 tbs grated chocolate

Mix the coffee with the brandy in a shallow dish. Dip half of the sponge fingers very briefly into the mixture to moisten them, then use to line the bottom of a glass bowl. Mix together the mascarpone, yogurt and ricotta until smooth, and add the sugar and vanilla. Whisk the egg whites until stiff and fold into the cheese mixture. Spoon half of this over the layer of sponge fingers. Make a second layer of moistened sponge fingers and cover with the rest of the cheese mixture. Sprinkle grated chocolate on top, cover and chill for several hours before serving.

CHOCOLATE DELIGHT

This sumptuous dessert of sherry-moistened sponge surrounding a rich chocolate mousse filling, all covered with whipped cream, is always a huge success. Everyone asks for the recipe, so here it is!

FOR 8–10

½ pint (300 ml) milk	6 free-range eggs, separated
a dash of sherry	8oz (250g) plain chocolate
8oz (250g) trifle sponges, split in half horizontally	½ pint (300ml) double cream, whipped
6oz (175g) margarine	grated plain chocolate to decorate
4oz (125g) caster sugar	
pinch of salt	

Mix the milk with the sherry in a shallow dish. Dip the split trifle sponges in it briefly to moisten, then use to line a greased 8 inch (20 cm) soufflé dish. Line the sides first and then cover the bottom.

Cream the margarine with the sugar and salt until light and fluffy, then beat in the egg yolks. Beat until the mixture is pale yellow. Melt the chocolate in a bowl over hot water, or in the microwave. Gradually beat the chocolate into the egg yolk mixture. In another bowl, whisk the egg whites until very stiff and fold into the mixture. Pour into the sponge-lined dish, cover and chill for at least 24 hours.

Turn out, cover with whipped cream and decorate with grated chocolate.

CRÈME BRÛLÉE

This is a healthier version of a famous classic, using crème fraîche instead of double cream. To vary the dessert, put halved seeded grapes, redcurrants, sliced banana or pear in the bottom of each ramekin before pouring in the custard.

FOR 6

1¼ lb (625g) crème fraîche	3 tbs caster sugar
thinly pared rind of 1 lemon, cut into thin strips	a few drops of vanilla essence
4 egg yolks from size-1 free-range eggs	6 tbs light soft brown sugar

Simmer the crème fraîche with the lemon rind gently for 10 minutes. Leave to cool for 10 minutes. Beat the egg yolks with the caster sugar in a heat-proof bowl until pale and creamy, add the vanilla essence and then strain in the crème fraîche, stirring well. Place the bowl over a pan of hot – not boiling – water and cook for 20–25 minutes or until the custard thickens, stirring occasionally. Don't let the water come to boiling point at any stage. When ready, the custard will be velvety in consistency and will lightly coat the back of a spoon. Put into 6 ramekin dishes and chill overnight.

The next day, sprinkle 1 tbs light brown sugar over the top of each custard and smooth evenly. Place under a very hot grill for 3–4 minutes or until the sugar has melted and is bubbling. Leave to cool, then chill again for up to 8 hours.

NEXT SPREAD: (left to right) Crème Brûlée, Redcurrant Cheesecake, Chocolate Delight and Pecan Pie

REDCURRANT CHEESECAKE

A very easy uncooked cheesecake, this is simply fresh redcurrants folded into cheese and whipped cream, on a crunchy biscuit base. Other soft fruits in season, such as raspberries, blackcurrants, sliced strawberries and blueberries, can be used instead of redcurrants.

FOR 6–8

6oz (175g) digestive biscuits	*½ pint (300ml) double cream, whipped*
2oz (50g) margarine, melted	
2lb (1kg) low fat soft cheese	*8oz (250g) redcurrants, topped and tailed*
6oz (175g) light soft brown sugar	

Crumble the biscuits finely (you can use a food processor for this if you have one). Add the melted margarine and mix thoroughly. Press evenly over the bottom of a greased 8 inch (20 cm) loose-bottomed flan tin. Chill until set.

Beat the soft cheese with the sugar until creamy. Fold in the whipped cream, then carefully fold in the redcurrants. Pile on to the prepared base and smooth the surface. Chill for several hours, or overnight, before serving.

PECAN PIE

A great American classic, this recipe brings out the best in the delicious pecan nut. Serve warm or at room temperature, with thick cream.

FOR 6

6oz (175g) sweetcrust pastry (see page 179)	*1 tbs plain flour*
	¼ pint (150ml) golden syrup
2oz (50g) margarine	*5 tbs skimmed milk*
4oz (125g) light soft brown sugar	*1 tsp vanilla essence*
	6oz (175g) shelled pecan nuts
2 free-range eggs, beaten	

Roll out the pastry dough and line an 8 inch (20 cm) loose-bottomed flan tin. Bake blind until part cooked (see page 115).

Cream the margarine with the sugar until light and fluffy, then beat in the eggs. Beat in the flour, syrup and milk. Add the vanilla and beat thoroughly until the mixture is light.

Sprinkle the nuts over the bottom of the pastry case and pour the mixture over them. Bake at 190°C/375°F/gas 5 for 15 minutes, then turn the heat down to 170°C/325°F/gas 3 and continue baking for 30 minutes or until a knife inserted in the centre comes out clean.

LEMON SOUFFLÉ TART

*A*party piece, this is complicated to make but a stunning finale to a special meal. It is intensely lemony, incredibly light, and needs only a little single cream to go with it.

FOR 12

8oz (250g) sweetcrust pastry (see page 179)	¼ pint (150ml) fresh lemon juice
4 size-1 free-range eggs, separated	2oz (50g) margarine
	pinch of salt
8oz (250g) caster sugar	2 tbs icing sugar

Roll out the pastry dough and line an 11 inch (28 cm) loose-bottomed flan tin. Bake blind (see page 115) at 220°C/425°F/gas 7 for 15 minutes, then uncover and bake for a further 5 minutes. Cool on a rack.

Beat the egg yolks with half of the caster sugar until thick and pale, then stir in the lemon juice. Put into a heavy-bottomed saucepan and heat gently, gradually adding the margarine. Stir constantly, being careful not to overheat to simmering point, until the mixture thickens. Cool, then chill for 1–2 hours.

Whisk the egg whites with the salt until they make soft peaks. Whisk in the remaining caster sugar 1 tbs at a time and continue whisking until the mixture is stiff and glossy.

Fold one-quarter of the egg whites into the lemon mixture, then carefully fold in the rest. Pour into the baked pastry case and bake at 190°C/375°F/gas 5 for 15 minutes or until the filling is puffed and light golden brown. Cool on a wire rack for at least 1 hour. Just before serving sift the icing sugar over the top.

BAKEWELL TART

*O*ne of the great traditional recipes of England, this tart consistently lives up to its excellent reputation. Serve it warm or at room temperature.

FOR 8

12oz (350g) sweetcrust pastry (see page 179)	8oz (250g) caster sugar
	8oz (250g) ground almonds
4-5 tbs raspberry jam	1oz (25g) plain flour
8oz (250g) margarine	4 free-range eggs, beaten

Roll out the pastry dough and line a 12 inch (30 cm) loose-bottomed flan tin. Spread the jam evenly over the bottom. Cream the margarine with the sugar until light and fluffy, then beat in the almonds and add the sifted flour. Beat in the eggs until the mixture is light and smooth. Spread in the pastry case.

Bake at 190°C/375°F/gas 5 for 45 minutes, watching towards the end in case it darkens too much. (You can cover the top with a piece of foil if it begins to burn.) Cool on a rack.

PEACH OR PLUM COBBLER

A fruit cobbler epitomizes the best of home cooking. You can use other fruits besides peaches or plums – apples, pears, gooseberries and so on. Delicious served with whipped cream or ice cream. It is a great American classic pudding.

FOR 6

2lb (1kg) ripe peaches, skinned, or plums, stones removed	For the cobbler topping:
	6oz (175g) plain flour
	pinch of salt
1-2 tbs sugar	1oz (25g) caster sugar
1 tsp grated lemon rind	1 tsp baking powder
1 tbs fresh lemon juice	½oz (40g) margarine
	1 free-range egg, beaten
	2 tbs skimmed milk or single cream

Slice the stoned fruit and put into a baking dish with sugar to taste and the lemon rind and juice.

To make the topping, sift the dry ingredients into a bowl and rub in the margarine until it resembles fine breadcrumbs. Fold in the beaten egg and then the milk or cream to bind to a light dough. Knead for a few moments. Divide the dough into 8 portions and shape each into a flat patty. Place them over the top of the fruit. Bake at 200°C/400°F/gas 6 for 25–30 minutes or until the cobbler topping is golden brown. Serve warm.

Skinning Peaches

Put peaches into a large bowl and cover with boiling water. Leave to stand for about 5 minutes. Lift out one by one and pierce the skin with a sharp knife; the skin will peel off easily.

BLUEBERRY TART

Here a sweet almond pastry case holds a rich blueberry filling topped with sweetened yogurt. The blueberries aren't cooked, so they keep their shape as well as their vitamins. If you prefer, you can make a more traditional blueberry pie following the recipe for apple pie on page 170.

FOR 6

12oz (350g) Austrian shortcrust pastry (see page 179)	½ pint (300ml) water
	2lb (1kg) blueberries
	2-3 tbs icing sugar
6oz (175g) granulated sugar	8fl oz (250ml) plain Greek yogurt
3 tbs cornflour	
pinch of salt	

Roll out the pastry dough and line a 9inch (22.5cm) pie tin, pressing in the pastry evenly with your knuckles. Bake blind (see page 115) at 190°C/375°F/gas 5 for 20 minutes, then uncover and crisp up for a further 5 minutes. Leave to cool.

Mix together the sugar, cornflour, salt and water in a saucepan and heat gently, stirring, until thick and smooth. Simmer gently for 5 minutes. Add half of the blueberries at a time and mix thoroughly. Cool.

Just before serving, pour the blueberry mixture into the cooked pastry case. Sift the icing sugar into the yogurt, stir well and spoon over the top of the tart just before serving.

OPPOSITE: Plum Cobbler

APPLE SPONGE PUDDING

*H*ere, tender sugar-glazed apples are baked on a sweet sponge base – an ideal pudding for chilly, damp days. Serve with whipped cream or pouring cream.

FOR 4–6

4 oz (125g) caster sugar	*1½ tsp baking powder*
1 size-1 free-range egg	*½ tsp ground cloves (optional)*
2 oz (50g) margarine	*12 oz (350g) cooking apples*
5 tbs skimmed or soya milk	*lemon juice*
3 oz (75g) plain flour	

Reserve ½ oz (15 g) of the sugar; put the remaining sugar in a bowl with the egg and whisk until thick and creamy. Heat the margarine and milk in a saucepan and bring to the boil. Pour into the egg and sugar mixture, whisking. Sift together the flour, baking powder and optional cloves and fold into the egg mixture, making sure there are no lumps of flour. Pour the mixture into a greased 9 x 6 inch (22.5 x 15 cm) baking tin.

Peel and core the apples and cut into slices. Arrange on top of the sponge mixture, leaving no gaps. Sprinkle with lemon juice and then with the reserved sugar. Bake at 200°C/400°F/gas 6 for about 40 minutes or until well risen and golden brown. Serve hot or leave to cool before serving, cut into slices.

APPLE PIE

*T*he best apple pies in the world are made with Bramleys, if you can get hold of them. But this pie is a treat at any time of the year, made with whatever apples are in season. Serve with thick yogurt or custard – or both!

FOR 4–6

12 oz (350g) sweetcrust pastry (see page 179)	*2-3 oz (50-75g) caster sugar*
	3 cloves
2 oz (50g) ground almonds	*1 oz (25g) margarine*
1½ lb (750g) apples, preferably Bramleys, peeled and cored	*beaten free-range egg to glaze*

Butter a 9–10 inch (22.5–25 cm) flan dish or pie tin. Roll out half of the pastry dough and line the dish.

Sprinkle with the ground almonds – they mop up the juices and stop the pastry going soggy. Slice the apples very thinly in the food processor and arrange in the pastry case, sprinkling with sugar to taste as you go. Tuck the cloves into the fruit and dot with the margarine.

Moisten the edge of the pastry case. Roll out the rest of the pastry dough and lay over the top. Press the edges together with a fork to seal them. Trim. Make a few slits in the pastry lid and brush the top with beaten egg. Bake at 220°C/425°F/gas 7 for 30–35 minutes or until the pastry is lightly browned. Serve hot or cold.

SPONGE PUDDING WITH APRICOTS AND ALMONDS

One of the simplest recipes ever, this is a family favourite at any time of year. If fresh apricots aren't in season, you can substitute canned apricot halves or dried apricots that have been soaked until plump and tender. Other fruits can replace the apricots: plums, peaches, nectarines and bananas for example.

FOR 3–4

12 oz (350 g) ripe but firm apricots, halved and stones removed	*2 oz (50 g) soft light brown sugar*
	1 size-1 free-range egg
	½ tsp vanilla essence
For the sponge topping:	*milk if needed*
2 oz (50 g) self-raising flour	*2 oz (50 g) flaked almonds,*
2 oz (50 g) margarine	*toasted and roughly chopped*

To make the sponge topping, sift the flour into a bowl and add the margarine, sugar, egg and vanilla essence. Beat together until light and creamy. If the mixture seems a little dry, add a small amount of milk. Stir in the almonds.

Arrange the apricots in a 1 pint (600 ml) baking dish and cover with the sponge topping. Bake at 170°C/325°F/gas 3 for 30–35 minutes or until the topping is well risen and golden brown. Serve hot, with cream or custard.

The Electric Mixer

This is indispensable for making cakes and biscuits, as well as many desserts. It beats air into a mixture in a way that even the strongest of wrists cannot!

FLOATING ISLANDS

No one can resist this pudding of tender poached meringue 'islands' floating on a custard 'sea'. The custard is stabilized with cornflour, which will prevent any curdling.

FOR 6–8

1¾ pints (1 litre) milk	*½ tsp vanilla or almond essence, or ¼ tsp ground mixed spice*
3 free-range eggs, separated	
4 oz (125 g) caster sugar	
1 tbs cornflour	*seedless raspberry jam*
½ tsp salt	

Heat the milk in a wide saucepan. Meanwhile, put 2 of the egg whites in a bowl and whisk until frothy. Add 2 tbs of the sugar and whisk until stiff.

Drop large heaping spoonfuls of the egg whites on to the hot milk, to make 6 or 8 meringues. Poach gently until the meringues feel just firm to the touch, turning them over so that they are cooked on both sides, about 2 minutes each side. When they are ready, remove with a slotted spoon and drain on paper towels. Reserve the hot milk.

Combine the remaining sugar, cornflour and salt in a bowl and stir to mix. Add the remaining egg white and the egg yolks and mix together until smoothly blended. Pour in the hot milk, stirring. Pour the custard mixture into the top of a double boiler set over simmering water, or into a heavy-based saucepan, and cook until thickened, stirring constantly. Remove from the heat and cool slightly, then stir in the essence or spice. Pour the custard into a wide serving dish and leave to cool completely. Before serving, arrange the meringues on top of the custard and dot with raspberry jam.

CARROT CAKE WITH CREAM CHEESE FROSTING

This rich carrot cake is made with cooked puréed carrots, which makes it deliciously moist, and it has some coconut and walnuts in it as well to add texture. Wonderful at teatime, and also as a dessert.

FOR 10–12

8oz (250g) plain flour	*1lb (500g) cooked carrots, puréed*
8oz (250g) light soft brown sugar	*4oz (125g) walnuts, chopped*
pinch of salt	*2oz (50g) desiccated coconut*
1 tsp baking powder	
2 tsp ground cinnamon	For the cream cheese frosting:
6 fl oz (175ml) sunflower oil	
2 free-range eggs, lightly beaten	*8oz (250g) low fat soft cheese*
	8oz (250g) icing sugar
1 tsp vanilla essence	*1 tbs fresh lemon juice*

Sift the dry ingredients into a bowl. Add the oil, eggs and vanilla and beat well. The mixture will be quite sticky. Beat in the carrots, mixing thoroughly. Fold in the walnuts and coconut.

Pour into a greased 8 inch (20 cm) cake tin and bake at 180°C/350°F/gas 4 for 1¼ hours or until a sharp knife inserted into the centre comes out clean. Cool on a rack.

To make the cream cheese frosting, mash the cheese and slowly sift in the icing sugar, beating until fully incorporated. Stir in the lemon juice.

When the cake is cold, cut it in half horizontally and fill with one-third of the cream cheese frosting. Spread the remaining frosting over the top and sides of the cake.

VEGAN FRUIT CAKE ♥

This rich, dark, moist cake contains no sugar, just a little golden syrup, relying instead on the natural sweetness of the dried fruits and fruit juice. Wrapped tightly and stored in an airtight tin, the cake will keep very well.

MAKES a 9½ x 6 inch (24 x 15 cm) cake

12oz (320g) sultanas	*16 fl oz (500ml) unsweetened orange juice*
9oz (280g) currants	
14oz (400g) glacé cherries, halved	*8 fl oz (250ml) soya milk*
	8oz (250g) wholemeal plain flour
5oz (150g) raisins, chopped	
2 tbs chopped glacé ginger (optional)	*8oz (250g) wholemeal self-raising flour*
4 tbs golden syrup	*2 tsp ground mixed spice*
3½oz (90g) margarine	

Combine the fruits, ginger, golden syrup, margarine and fruit juice in a large saucepan. Stir over a low heat until the margarine has melted, then cover the pan and simmer for 5 minutes. Pour the fruit mixture into a large bowl and leave to cool to room temperature.

Add the soya milk and stir to mix. Sift the flours and spice into the bowl (tip in the bran left in the sieve) and mix thoroughly.

Pour the cake mixture into a greased 9½ x 6 inch (24 x 15 cm) rectangular cake tin lined with 3 layers of greaseproof paper, and bake at 170°C/325°F/gas 3 for about 1½ hours or until a skewer inserted into the centre comes out clean. Leave to cool, in the tin, on a wire rack.

OPPOSITE: Carrot Cake with Cream Cheese Frosting

LEMON DRIZZLE CAKE

Light but very moist, this lemony cake is perfect for special occasions. Ice with the cream cheese frosting on page 172 for a birthday cake.

MAKES a 9 x 5 inch (23 x 13 cm) cake

4oz (125g) margarine	*6oz (175g) plain flour*
5oz (150g) caster sugar	*2 tsp baking powder*
finely grated rind and juice of 3 lemons	*4 tbs skimmed milk*
	2oz (50g) granulated sugar
2 size-1 free-range eggs, beaten	

Cream the margarine with the caster sugar, lemon rind and 1½ tbs of the lemon juice until light and fluffy. Beat in the eggs one at a time. Beat in the sifted flour and baking powder, then add the milk. Beat thoroughly until light. Put into a greased 2 lb (1 kg) loaf tin and bake at 180°C/350°F/gas 4 for 45 minutes.

Towards the end of the baking time, heat the remaining lemon juice with the granulated sugar until the sugar dissolves. Simmer for 3–4 minutes.

Cool the cake, in the tin, on a rack for 5 minutes, then turn out, upside down. Pierce the base of the cake all over with a skewer, being careful not to break through the top surface of the cake. Spoon the lemon syrup carefully over the base of the cake until all of it has been absorbed. Leave to cool completely before turning the cake right way up.

CHOCOLATE VICTORIA SPONGE WITH CHOCOLATE BUTTER ICING

*T*his light chocolate sponge, filled and iced with chocolate butter icing, never fails to please. It is easy to make too.

FOR 8

4oz (125g) plain flour	For the chocolate butter
2 tsp baking powder	icing:
2 tbs cocoa powder	
4oz (125g) caster sugar	*3oz (75g) margarine*
4oz (125g) margarine	*12oz (350g) icing sugar, sifted*
2 free-range eggs	*1 tbs cocoa powder*
1 tsp vanilla essence	*1-2 tbs strong black coffee*
	1½oz (40g) grated chocolate

Sift the flour, baking powder and cocoa into a large bowl. Add the caster sugar. Rub in the margarine until it resembles fine breadcrumbs. Beat in the eggs, beating until the mixture is very light. Add the vanilla and beat again.

Put the mixture into a greased 8 inch (20 cm) round loose-bottomed cake tin. Bake at 170°C/325°F/gas 3 for 30 minutes. Leave to cool in the tin for a couple of minutes, then carefully turn out on to a wire rack to cool completely.

To make the icing, cream the margarine with the sifted icing sugar and cocoa until well blended. Add enough coffee to make a spreadable consistency, then fold in the grated chocolate.

When the cake is cold, cut it in half horizontally and fill with one-third of the chocolate butter icing. Cover the top and sides of the cake with the remaining icing.

OPPOSITE: Lemon Drizzle Cake

CRISPY GINGER NUTS ♥

These gingery biscuits have some crystallized ginger in them which gives a touch of softness in contrast to the crisp bite. They freeze perfectly.

MAKES 18

3oz (75g) self-raising flour	3oz (75g) margarine
3oz (75g) wholemeal flour	2 tbs caster sugar
2½ tsp baking powder	1½ rounded tbs golden syrup, heated gently
½ tsp bicarbonate of soda	
1½ tsp ground cinnamon	2oz (50g) crystallized ginger, chopped small
3 tsp ground ginger	

Sift the dry ingredients into a bowl (tip in the bran left in the sieve). Rub in the margarine until it resembles fine breadcrumbs. Mix in the sugar, then the warmed golden syrup and the crystallized ginger. Knead to a light dough.

Break off small pieces of dough the size of a walnut, shape into balls and put on to a greased baking sheet. Flatten the balls with a fork. Bake at 200°C/400°F/gas 6 for 12 minutes. Cool on the baking sheet for 5 minutes, then lift carefully on to a rack to cool completely.

CHOCOLATE CHIP COOKIES

These ever-popular cookies have the richness of chocolate and the crunch of nuts (pecans have been suggested, although you could also use walnuts or hazelnuts). They freeze extremely well.

MAKES 10 large or 15 medium

4oz (125g) margarine	8oz (250g) plain flour
2oz (50g) caster sugar	1 tsp baking powder
4oz (125g) light soft brown sugar	½ tsp salt
	6oz (175g) chocolate chips
1 free-range egg, beaten	4oz (125g) pecan nuts, roughly chopped
1 tsp vanilla essence	

Cream the margarine with both of the sugars until light and fluffy. Beat in the egg. Add the vanilla. Sift the flour with the baking powder and salt, and sift again into the bowl. Beat well to mix. Fold in the chocolate chips and the nuts.

Drop spoonfuls of the dough on to a well-greased baking sheet, leaving space around each to allow for spreading. Bake at 190°C/375°F/gas 5 for 15 minutes or until lightly browned. Cool on the baking sheet for 5 minutes before lifting carefully on to a rack to cool completely.

OAT AND RAISIN BISCUITS

Great family favourites, these are spiced with a hint of cinnamon. They are delicious with a glass of milk or juice or a cup of tea or coffee.

MAKES 10

2oz (50g) margarine	*½ tsp salt*
4oz (125g) light soft brown sugar	*½ tsp baking powder*
	1 tsp ground cinnamon
1 free-range egg	*6oz (175g) porridge oats*
1 tsp vanilla essence	*4oz (125g) raisins*
2oz (50g) plain flour	

Cream the margarine with the sugar until light and fluffy. Beat in the egg. Add the vanilla. Sift the flour with the salt, baking powder and cinnamon, then beat into the egg mixture. Add the oats and raisins and mix thoroughly together.

Drop spoonfuls of dough on to well-greased baking sheets, leaving space around each to allow for spreading. Bake at 180°C/350°F/gas 4 for 15 minutes. Allow to cool on the baking sheet for 5 minutes, then lift carefully on to a rack to cool completely.

ABOVE: (left to right) Chocolate Chip Cookies, Crispy Ginger Nuts, Oat and Raisin Biscuits

CHAPTER TEN

Pastry Basics

FLAKY PASTRY ⓥ

MAKES 14 oz (400 g)

8oz (250g) plain flour	*6oz (175g) margarine*
pinch of salt	*4-6 tbs cold water*

Sift the flour with the salt into a bowl and rub in 2 oz (50 g) of the margarine. Add enough water to bind lightly. Turn on to a floured board and knead until smooth.

Roll out into an oblong. Cover the top of the dough with half of the remaining margarine, in knobs, then fold the dough into three (the bottom third up and the top third down). Moisten the side edges with water and press to seal. Give the dough a quarter turn so that these edges are at the top and bottom. Roll out again into an oblong and repeat the process, using the remaining margarine. Chill for 10–15 minutes, then roll out and fold into three once more. The dough is now ready to use as required. Bake at 220°C/425°F/gas 7.

PUFF PASTRY ⓥ

MAKES 1 lb (500 g)

8oz (250g) plain flour	*¼ pint (150ml) ice cold water*
pinch of salt	*squeeze of fresh lemon juice*
8oz (250g) margarine	

Sift the flour with the salt into a bowl and rub in a walnut-size piece of margarine. Bind with the water and lemon juice and knead to make a smooth dough. Chill for 15 minutes.

Roll out the dough to an oblong. Place the margarine, in a block, in the centre. Wrap the dough around the margarine like a parcel and turn over. **Roll out to an oblong again, fold in three (the bottom third up and the top third down) and press the side edges to seal them. Give the dough a quarter turn so that these edges are at the top and bottom.** Repeat from ** to **. Wrap in greaseproof paper or a teacloth and chill for 15 minutes. Repeat from ** to ** six more times, chilling between each of these 'turns'. Chill for 10 minutes before rolling out finally for baking. Bake at 220°C/425°F/gas 7.

EASY SHORTCRUST PASTRY ⱽ

MAKES 9 oz (275 g)

3oz (75g) margarine	*6oz (175g) plain flour*
large pinch of fine sea salt	*3 tbs cold water*

Put all the ingredients into the blender or food processor and blend until amalgamated and crumbly. Knead to a smooth dough on a floured board, then chill for at least 30 minutes before using.

If you don't have a blender or food processor, sift the flour with the salt into a bowl and rub in the margarine, lifting the mixture to incorporate as much air as possible. When the mixture resembles fine breadcrumbs, bind with the water. Knead on a floured board until smooth.

AUSTRIAN SHORTCRUST PASTRY

MAKES 1 lb (500 g)

5oz (150g) margarine	*3oz (75g) ground almonds*
5oz (150g) plain flour	*1 free-range egg yolk*
3oz (75g) caster sugar	*1 tsp grated lemon rind*

Rub the margarine lightly into the sifted flour until the mixture resembles fine breadcrumbs. Stir in the sugar and ground almonds. Mix in the egg yolk and lemon rind and knead on a lightly floured board until smooth. Chill for 30 minutes. When using, roll out to ¼ inch (6mm) thickness.

SWEETCRUST PASTRY ⱽ

MAKES 12 oz (350 g)

8oz (250g) plain flour	*4oz (125g) margarine*
1 tbs caster sugar	*3 tbs cold water*

Sift the flour into a large bowl and stir in the sugar. Rub in the margarine lightly until the mixture resembles fine breadcrumbs. Bind with the water. Knead lightly on a floured board until smooth. Wrap and chill for at least 30 minutes before rolling out.

179

Vegetarian Questions and Answers

Q What is a vegetarian and what is a vegan?

A A vegetarian is someone who doesn't eat meat, fish, poultry or any animal. Vegetarians don't eat any foods containing the by-products of slaughter such as gelatine (which is ground-up bones, hooves, hides etc) or animal rennet (which is prepared from the stomach lining of calves and used in the making of many non-vegetarian cheeses) or lard or suet (the hard waxy fat from the kidneys and loins of sheep and cattle).

A vegetarian diet is based on the foods of the fields – grains, pulses, nuts, seeds, vegetables and fruit – as is a vegan diet. The difference between vegetarians and vegans is that veggies eat eggs, cheese and other dairy products, whereas vegans eat none of these.

Q What are the reasons for not eating meat?

A For me, the main reason has always been my love of animals. Because of that love, I don't want any animal to die for my plate.

A lot of people who turn vegetarian feel the same – factory farming methods appal them, as do the way that animals are slaughtered and the way they are transported to their slaughter.

Others are rightfully wary of the large doses of hormones and antibiotics that are pumped into many animals, and wary too of the effects of the pesticides that are used on animal feed.

The other big reason for not eating meat is health. More and more surveys suggest that a vegetarian diet can help reduce your risk of cancer, heart disease, diabetes, high blood pressure and other illnesses. This is partly because vegetarian meals tend to be lower in fat and also because there is no cholesterol in vegetables – only food from animals contains cholesterol.

There's also the matter of the health of the planet to think about. This earth needs all the trees it can get in order to breathe properly and yet millions of acres are hacked down to clear grazing for cattle and sheep. Many people are now finding it unacceptable that, in order to bring beef to their plates, a huge acreage of Central and South American rain forest has been cleared to provide grazing land for cattle. At a time when tree cover of this earth is reducing rapidly, kids need to know that for every quarterpounder made from Central or South American beef, six square yards of rainforest are hewn for pasture.

As the inheritors of the planet, our children also need to know that they and their children will be facing the prospect of a dramatic decline in fresh water tables principally because of the billions of gallons used each year to rear livestock. For instance, 70 per cent of all fresh American water is used in agriculture, and whereas it takes 25 gallons of that water to produce a pound of wheat, it takes an astonishing 5,214 gallons to produce a pound of beef! (Source: University of California)

Q Is a meatless diet a healthy diet?

A Absolutely. It's balanced, it's nutritious and you're getting the goodness direct from the vegetables and fruit instead of via an animal. Also, as I've said, because it is lower in saturated fat and cholesterol, there are fewer worries about your heart and your weight. Not only is this way of eating healthy, another advantage is that you'll *feel* healthier because your body is not working overtime trying to digest all that meat. You don't feel sluggish, you've got much more get up and go.

Q Will I get enough protein if I don't eat meat?

A Yes, more than enough. It's one of the great myths that vegetarians don't get enough protein from their food. The opposite is the case, even for children – we tend to eat *too much* protein. A balanced diet of fresh vegetables, fruit, nuts and pulses will provide your daily protein needs.

Q What IS a healthy diet?

A One that keeps you well. Generally, a healthy diet should be low in saturated fats, low in cholesterol, high in fibre and carbohydrates, low in refined sugar and rich in minerals and vitamins. By using fresh vegetables and fruit in your cooking, you'll achieve this – *and* you'll have a healthy mind: your conscience is clear because nothing died for you today.

Q I want to slim. Is it possible to diet and lose weight in a healthy vegetarian way?

A Yes, and very enjoyably: by eating large amounts of fresh vegetables and fruit and cutting back on your dairy intake you'll get all the nutrients you need – minus the calories. You'll have a high-fibre diet – so you won't feel as hungry – and you'll find it a very tasty way to lose weight.

Q What would happen to the animals if nobody ate them?

A They'd be a lot happier, for a start. It's certainly not true that we'd be over-run with animals. There are so many "food" animals on the planet because they are over-bred by humans. For instance, in a farmyard a sow will produce about six piglets a year, but intensive farming has interfered with her to the extent that she can now produce 20 piglets a year. That's not natural.

Pigs, cows, and sheep are not going to become extinct if people stop eating them. To my knowledge, no species of animal has died out simply because humans stopped killing it.

Nature balances her own, she doesn't need us to interfere.

Q How many people are vegetarian?

A In six words – millions and more by the minute.

Few people in the West stop to think that vegetarianism is a way of life for vast numbers of people – all the tens of millions of Hindus and Buddhists for a start. There have been vegetarians on this planet since human life began – in fact the recent discovery of the oldest human fossil, in East Africa in 1994, indicates that Early Man (*Homo rudolfiensis*) was strictly vegetarian. Examination of the contents of his stomach revealed he lived entirely on a diet of grains, nuts and vegetables.

As far back as the 6th century BC, Pythagoras was advocating vegetarianism and many of the greatest thinkers since have been vegetarians, as were Plotinus, Plutarch, Diogenes and Ovid. So too was Buddha. In fact,

it is interesting to note that many of the great minds that have shaped civilization belonged to vegetarians – people like Luther, Alexander Pope, Shelley, Thoreau, Gandhi, Milton, Da Vinci, Voltaire, Wordsworth, Tolstoy, Blake and Benjamin Franklin. And people like George Bernard Shaw, who said: "While we ourselves are the living graves of murdered beasts, how can we expect any ideal conditions on this earth?"

Now, many people in the UK and USA are heeding Shaw's wisdom. In the UK, seven per cent of the population are declared veggies. More than 10 per cent of British students are vegetarian and the numbers are growing daily, especially among young girls – in one recent survey of teenage schoolgirls, 57 per cent of those aged under 14 said they were vegetarian. In the USA the number of vegetarians has almost *doubled* over the past ten years from 6.5 million to 12.4 million.

Also a recent official report by the Frozen Food Information Service on hot-food trends in the 21st century estimated that during the next decade as many as 20 per cent of the people in Britain may become vegetarian.

So there are quite a few of us.

Q Is it safe to bring up children on a meatless diet?

A Totally safe. I looked into this with a nutritionist when we first went veggie, and providing your children are fed a balanced diet with enough protein, minerals and vitamins – preferably from fresh vegetables and fruit – and in the case of younger children some fat for energy, they can be vegetarians from birth.

Q Are desserts always vegetarian?

A No, check the labels for gelatine, the base of most fruit jelly, and for rennet and whey. Processed desserts may contain some emulsifiers (see What should I look for on labels?, below). Safest of all, make your own desserts – they'll probably be tastier.

Q What do I say to my friends?

A You could try saying what I do when I cook them a meal: "Try this, you'll love it." There is no reason for any vegetarian to feel apologetic about what he or she chooses to eat. Personally, I think the reasons I've listed above are more than good enough reasons not to eat animals but, if you feel peer pressure, maybe you could say what one of my daughters said when she was asked how she felt about not eating meat. She said, "I feel like I have a clear conscience."

Q How will I fit in with family meals?

A You'll fit in fine because vegetarian cooking is so simple. If the family meal consists of the traditional meat and two veg then just leave the meat off your plate and fill the gap with either a cheese or egg dish or any of the meatless meals such as veggie sausages, burgers, pies and pastas that are available today.

But once you get into this new way of eating I bet you'll find that the meals are so tasty and healthy that before long other members of your family will want to try them too.

Q What about eating out in restaurants or entertaining friends?

A You'll have a good choice these days. Italian, Chinese, Indian and Mexican restaurants are ideal as many of their traditional dishes are meatless anyway. Even French restaurants usually have mushroom, rice or egg dishes to choose from.

As for eating with friends – if you're cooking, be proud to be veggie and be adventurous. There are dishes in this book to suit every appetite, and don't feel you'll be alienating your friends because, while many people do eat meat, I don't know of any who *only* eat meat. So, seeing vegetables on their plate is hardly going to be alien to them.

The other trick is not to tell them. With the abundance of meatless meals on the market, you can quite easily cook a meal that looks and tastes like meat.

Q Where do I buy meatless products?

A Although it used to be only health stores that stocked meatless meals, you'll find them widely available in any good supermarket chain. If your supermarket doesn't stock them, ask them to.

Q What's the difference between free-range eggs and other eggs?

A Free-range hens are just that – they can roam indoors or outdoors, they live as near to their natural state as possible and they have a balanced diet. They are not overcrowded and they are healthy.

Barn chickens are kept indoors in so-called barns without much daylight and in more crowded conditions than their free-ranging cousins.

Factory or battery hens are, in my opinion and in the opinion of most vegetarians, treated with great cruelty. They are cooped up in tiny spaces, frequently spending their entire lives in a wire cage. They are packed together, away from sunlight, and they often suffer deformities of the feet as they cannot move far and are forced to stand on wire netting. They are debeaked at birth to prevent them attacking each other in their madness. They are doped with large doses of antibiotics to prevent disease spreading in their overcrowded conditions and their lives are basically miserable. The picture of misery is made clear by an analogy provided by the Royal Society for the Prevention of Cruelty to Animals – which said that the space allocated to a hen in a battery hen house is the equivalent to stuffing a budgerigar into a jam jar.

Q Why should I eat organic products?

A I believe our food should be as natural as it is possible to grow it. I don't wish to eat fruit and vegetables that have been "bettered" with chemicals and pesticides – simply because I do not want, nor do I need, to have pesticides in my diet. I know that some fruit and vegetables are treated with substances to give them a longer shelf life or to make them look more attractive, but I'd rather have my food grown by Mother Nature than by the chemical industry.

Unfortunately there is currently little demand for organic produce. It is not always easily available, prices are quite high, and people have become accustomed to large and perfectly formed vegetables. However, it is up to the individual to create a greater demand, which will eventually bring about a reduction in cost.

Q What should I look for on labels to avoid animal products?

A It is surprising how many animal derivatives are contained in everyday products – your soap could contain lard, your biscuits animal fats – which is why it is important to check *all* labels.

Beware gelatine, the gelling agent found in many foods, which is produced from animal bones and hooves.

Watch out for whey, the liquid part of milk that remains after the separation of the curds by rennet – usually animal – during the cheese-making process.

If you need to take vitamins, make sure that the capsules are not made from gelatine and check that none of the ingredients is an animal derivative. In particular, avoid added vitamin D, which is often animal-derived. Vitamin D3 is taken from lanolin, from sheep's wool, but not necessarily from live sheep.

Watch out too for all emulsifiers in the E470 to E479 range (except E479a), as these can be derived from either animal or vegetable fats but it is not specified which.

Even your household products contain animal derivatives, so check these carefully. Lastly, your beauty products may contain collagen and glycerine, and these may be animal derivatives too.

Q Are meatless meals time-consuming to prepare?

A No, just the opposite. They are quick and simple to cook as vegetables require so much less cooking time than meat.

Q What can I feed to my dog?

A There are several brands of dried vegetarian dog food available, all carefully prepared to give a nutritional balance. The brand I am associated with is called Best. My dogs love it and I've had lots of letters from people telling me that Best has helped with their dog's stomach problems and skin conditions. Vets recommend it.

You can also give your pets wholesome bits of home cooking, but don't give them spicy foods as these may upset their stomachs, and avoid sugary foods as these will make them fat. Give dogs a piece of carrot or apple to chew on instead of a bone.

Q Isn't meatless food boring?

A Not if you like good, healthy, tasty and colourful food. Because of what we *don't* eat, vegetarianism is about *life*, saving it and enjoying it. That shouldn't be boring. Anyway, try any recipe in this book and see for yourself.

Q What foods shall I keep in store and how do I prepare them?

A Read the following pages!

The Vegetarian Pantry

Basic Processed Foods

- canned tomatoes
- canned sweetcorn
- canned beans: cannellini, butter, red kidney, borlotti, flageolet etc
- canned baked beans
- pasta: wholemeal and plain
- wholemeal bread
- soya products: soya milk, tofu, tempeh, vegetarian mince, vegetarian steak chunks, soy sauce, tamari
- vegetable stock cubes
- vegetarian gravy mix
- Marmite, yeast extract
- curry powder
- tomato purée
- tomato ketchup, pickles, relishes, chutneys, mustards
- mayonnaise
- Oriental sauces: black bean, garlic, yellow bean, etc
- Mexican taco sauces and relishes

Frozen Products

- there is now a wide range of readymade frozen vegetarian meals available from supermarkets, including my own brand. These convenient products are ideal for busy cooks

Dairy Products

- free-range eggs
- vegetarian cheese
- plain yogurt

Spreads, Oils and Vinegars

- polyunsaturated margarine (read the label for hidden animal products)
- tahini
- vegetable pastes
- vinegars: cider, wine, rice, balsamic
- olive oil
- vegetable oils: sunflower, grapeseed, soya, groundnut
- dark sesame oil
- walnut oil
- honey, jams (low sugar and homemade), maple syrup

Cereals

- barley, buckwheat, cornmeal, millet, oats, wheat
- rice
- wild rice
- unbleached organic flour

Dried Fruit

- raisins, sultanas, currants
- apples
- apricots
- glacé cherries
- mixed peel
- peaches
- pears
- prunes

Dried Pulses

- dried beans: black, black-eye, borlotti, butter, haricot, flageolet, mung, red kidney, soya
- lentils: red, green, brown
- split peas
- chick peas

Basic Plant Foods

- nuts: almonds, brazils, cashews, hazelnuts, peanuts, pecans, pine kernels, pistachios, walnuts
- seeds: pumpkin, sesame, sunflower, poppy
- dried coconut
- capers
- olives
- sun-dried tomatoes
- chillies: dried and in brine

Herbs and Spices

- sea salt, peppercorns
- vanilla: pods, essence
- herbal teas
- the complete range: fresh and dried herbs, whole and ground spices, to your taste

Fruit and Vegetables

- plenty of fresh, organic fruit and vegetables
- in season

Pulses

Pulses, which include beans, peas and lentils, are very versatile, and they are an excellent source of protein, carbohydrate, vitamins and minerals, as well as being low in fat and high in fibre. The soya bean is the best source of quality protein.

Dried pulses need to be soaked overnight, in plenty of water to cover, before cooking. The exceptions are lentils and split peas: large whole lentils and large split peas need only 2–3 hours soaking, and very small red lentils and small split peas need no soaking at all.

To cook pulses, drain off the soaking water and rinse them, then put into a saucepan and cover with fresh water. (If cooking red kidney beans, bring to the boil, boil for 10 minutes, then drain and put back in the pan with fresh cold water to cover.) Add a bay leaf and a slice or two of onion for extra flavour. Bring to the boil and simmer, covered, for the time given in the chart below. Wait to add salt until 10 minutes before the end of the cooking time – it toughens the skins and hardens them if you add it earlier.

Dried pulses double their weight after being soaked and cooked, so when using them instead of canned pulses in a recipe, use half the weight of the canned pulses given. In other words, for 8oz (250g) canned kidney beans, soak and cook 4oz (125g) dried kidney beans.

When using canned pulses in a recipe, it's best to add them towards the end of the cooking time so that they don't go mushy. Drain them well and rinse them under running cold water before you use them.

COOKING TIMES FOR PULSES, AFTER SOAKING

Aduki beans . . . . 30–60 minutes
Black-eye beans . . . . 1½ hours
Borlotti beans . . . . 1 hour
Butter beans . . . . 1–1½ hours
Cannellini beans . . . . 1 hour
Chick peas . . . . 1½–2 hours
Flageolets . . . . 45 minutes
Haricot beans . . . . 1–1½ hours
Lentils, large brown or green . . . . 45 minutes
Mung beans . . . . 40 minutes
Red kidney beans . . . . 1–1½ hours
Soya beans . . . . 3–4 hours
Split peas, large . . . . 40–50 minutes

COOKING TIMES FOR PULSES WHICH REQUIRE NO PRE-SOAKING

Lentils, small red . . . . 20–30 minutes
Split peas, small . . . . 45–60 minutes

Soya Products

The soya bean is the seed of the soya bean plant. It has been used as a staple in the Chinese diet for more than 4,000 years. From the soya bean come many soya products that are widely used in a vegetarian diet. These include:

• soya milk, which is made by soaking soya beans in water and then straining. Soya cheese and soya yogurt are made from soya milk.

• tofu, which is a curd made from coagulated soya milk. (Vegans can use tofu in place of yogurt in soups, dips, salad dressings and sauces. 'Silken' tofu, which is widely available, is light and creamy and works very well in all these recipes.)

• tempeh, which is a fermented soya bean paste made by mixing cooked soya beans with a fungus that holds it together.

• miso, which is a fermented condiment made from soya beans, grain (rice or barley), salt and water.

• soya or soy sauce (shoyu), which is made by fermenting soya beans with cracked roasted wheat, salt and water.

• tamari, which is another soy sauce, similar to shoyu but slightly stronger and made without wheat.

• soya margarine and soya oil, both of which are high in polyunsaturated fats and low in saturated fats
• soya flour
• TVP, or textured vegetable protein, which is de-fatted soya flour, processed and dried to provide a substance that has a spongy texture, similar to meat. A good source of fibre and high quality protein, TVP is also fortified with vitamin B12.

Wheat

Wheat protein, which is derived from wheat gluten, can be processed to resemble closely the texture of meat and is widely used as a meat substitute.

Cooking with Meat Substitutes

Meat substitutes are available as mince and chunks, as well as sausages and burgers. All can be found in supermarkets and health food stores. The joy of using vegetarian mince and chunks is that you can take them straight from the freezer – there's no need to thaw them. Just measure out the amount called for in the recipe and add it as directed. You can use them in curries, chilli non carne (see page 55), in a shepherd's pie (page 101) or a bolognese sauce (page 154) for spaghetti or lasagne – any dish where you would expect to find mince or stewing steak. (Readers in Great Britain can also find mince and chunks in chilled form – use them exactly as you would the frozen version.)

To brown vegetarian mince or steak chunks (which brings out their flavour), sauté them lightly in 2 tbs hot oil for each 8 oz (250 g). If you are in a hurry you can use these products without browning them first, although they will be slightly less tasty.

As a general rule, every 1 lb (500 g) mince or chunks needs at least ¾ pint (450 ml) liquid in their sauce since they are usually more absorbent than meat. Neither vegetarian mince nor chunks need much salt, so season judiciously.

Vegetarian Cheese

To make cheese, a substance called rennet is used to coagulate milk, separating it into curds and whey. The curds are treated to make cheese, and the liquid whey finds its way into margarines and many other products. Vegetarian cheese is made with rennets of non-animal origin.

Fig leaves, thistle, melon and safflower have provided the country housewife with plant rennets in the past, but today most vegetarian cheeses are made using rennet produced by a fungus, Mucor miehei, or from a bacteria (Bacillus subtilis). Animal rennet, which contains the enzyme chymosin, is usually obtained from the stomach of newly born calves. Advances in genetic engineering have led to the synthesizing of chymosin, which may soon replace animal rennet.

Vegetarian cheeses are usually clearly labelled. Vegetarian versions of cream cheese and other soft cheeses, Cheddar, Cheshire, double Gloucester, stilton, brie, dolcelatte and other blue cheeses, feta and ricotta can all be found in major supermarkets. Cottage cheese is always vegetarian. Parmesan is normally made with animal rennet, although a vegetarian version is emerging. Mozzarella is not always vegetarian.

Cheese is a good source of protein, as well as calcium, zinc, vitamin B12 and a little iron. New vegetarians should be wary of eating too much cheese as it contains a lot of saturated fat and can lead to high cholesterol levels.

Mushrooms

In some parts of the world gathering wild mushrooms is a national pastime, a family outing to harvest the ceps, chanterelles, boletus, parasol and field mushrooms that grow in the woods and fields at certain times of the year. Gathering mushrooms is a wonderful experience, akin to a treasure hunt, and you are well rewarded when you deliver them to the table.

Obviously you have to be careful not to pick the wrong ones, but the poisonous mushrooms are easily identifiable with a good field guide. So take to the woods and fields and enjoy the pleasures of both the hunt and the table.

Nutrition for Vegetarians

A good diet is a balanced diet: it is the overall mixture that counts. The important thing is to eat a wide variety of foods to give you the nutrients that the body needs to maintain growth, to repair itself, to provide energy, and to resist infection. At least once a day, everyone should eat a well-balanced meal, which means one that contains sufficient carbohydrate, protein, fat, dietary fibre, water, vitamins and minerals for individual needs. These dietary needs vary according to sex, age, activity levels, physical condition and climate. There are numerous books that give detailed information on this complex subject, but the guidelines here should help you ensure that you are getting a good nutritional balance in your daily diet.

Energy and Water

Food is the fuel that gives the human body energy, thus enabling it to work. The right amount of food is essential for normal biological processes such as breathing and pumping blood round the body, to perform muscular work and to maintain body temperature. Certain foods provide more energy than others; some provide it quickly while others release it slowly into the system.

Water comprises two-thirds of our body weight, and we cannot survive for more than a few days without water. Many foods contain high levels, but it is also important to drink sufficient water on a daily basis: experts suggest 1¾–3½ pints (1–2 litres) every day.

Protein

Proteins are made up from various combinations of amino acids that are required by our bodies for growth and repair. Both plant proteins and animal proteins contain these amino acids, so it is a fallacy that we can only get protein from an animal source. Excess amounts of protein cannot be stored in the body, so eating more than you need can have no benefit. In fact, it can be harmful – many western meat-eating diets contain far too much protein and this is now thought to cause diseases including certain cancers and osteoporosis, as well as poor kidney function.

A healthy, balanced diet containing a variety of foods will provide you with all the protein you require.

GOOD SOURCES OF PROTEIN Pulses (in particular soya beans), soya products (tofu, soya milk, etc), nuts, seeds, rice, pasta, wheat flour, bread, muesli, oatmeal, cheese, eggs, milk, yogurt, potatoes, peas, cauliflower, broccoli, garlic, sweetcorn.

Carbohydrate

Carbohydrate is a major source of energy in the diet, and most of it is provided by plant foods. There are three main types of carbohydrate in food: sugars, starches and cellulose. Cellulose is the indigestible part of plant foods and is the main constituent of dietary fibre. This stimulates the digestive system, helps prevent constipation and reduces the risk of colon cancer and diverticular disease.

GOOD SOURCES OF CARBOHYDRATE Pulses, rice, pasta, buckwheat groats, bulgar wheat, oatmeal, bread, nuts, potatoes, root vegetables, peas, sweetcorn, onions, garlic, dried apricots, bananas, mangoes.

GOOD SOURCES OF DIETARY FIBRE Pulses, nuts, wholemeal bread, wholemeal pasta, wheat bran, oats and other whole grains, most vegetables (particularly beans, cabbage, carrots, potatoes), raspberries, blackberries, redcurrants, dates, figs, prunes, dried apricots.

Fat and Cholesterol

Fat provides energy in a more concentrated form than carbohydrate and converts very easily into body fat. Although a certain amount of fat is necessary to provide warmth and essential nutrients and to protect the internal organs, the average western diet contains too much. Fats from animal sources contain a high proportion of saturated fatty acids, which raise blood cholesterol levels and increase the risk of heart disease.

Cholesterol is unique to animals and humans. It is made mainly in the liver and is present in all of the body's tissues. We need cholesterol but we do not necessarily need it in the diet: for some people an excess can cause health problems. This is why people on a diet containing no animal products are thought to be less at risk from heart disease.

SOURCES OF FAT Cheese, cream, yogurt, whole milk, butter, margarine, egg yolk, nuts, seeds, avocados, olives, vegetable oils, oats.

Vitamins

Small amounts of vitamins are essential for the regulation of all bodily processes. With the exception of vitamin D, the body cannot make its own vitamins, and some cannot be stored. Vitamins must therefore be obtained from food on a daily basis. A vegetarian diet can provide all the necessary vitamins.

VITAMIN A

Required for healthy skin and mucus membranes, and for night vision. Thought to help prevent the development of cancer.

GOOD SOURCES OF VITAMIN A Butter, margarine, milk, cheese, yogurt, cream, sweet potatoes, butternut squash, carrots, red peppers, chillies, leeks, lettuce, broccoli, Swiss chard, spinach, tomatoes, watercress, basil, coriander, parsley, apricots, cantaloupe melons, mangoes, papayas, guavas, sharon fruit.

B VITAMINS

A group of eight actual vitamins and several vitamin-like compounds. The main ones include:

Thiamin (B1): Releases energy from carbohydrate, alcohol and fat.

Riboflavin (B2): Releases energy from protein, fat and carbohydrate.

Niacin (B3): Involved in the oxidative release of energy from food; protects the skin and helps improve circulation.

Vitamin B6: Essential for protein metabolism, and for the formation of haemoglobin – the pigment in the blood that carries oxygen round the body.

Vitamin B12: Helps protect nerves and is involved in the formation of red blood cells in the bone marrow.

Folate: Involved in the formation of new cells and therefore essential for the normal growth and development of the foetus.

GOOD SOURCES OF B VITAMINS Eggs, cheese, milk, pulses, wholemeal bread, brown rice, fortified breakfast cereals, nuts, seeds, yeast extract, avocados, cauliflower, cabbage, peas, potatoes, mushrooms, green leafy vegetables, dates, figs, currants, dried apricots, clementines, canteloupe melon.

VITAMIN C

Essential for the formation of bones, teeth and tissues. Speeds the healing of wounds, helps maintain elasticity of the skin, aids the absorption of iron and improves resistance to infection. May help prevent the occurrence and development of cancer.

GOOD SOURCES OF VITAMIN C Broccoli, Brussels sprouts, cauliflower, cabbage, mangetout, green leafy vegetables, red peppers, chillies, watercress, parsley, blackcurrants, strawberries, kiwi fruit, guavas, citrus fruit.

NOTE: With the exception of niacin (B3), these vitamins are easily destroyed by heat. Vitamin C is easily destroyed by exposure to air, and all are unstable in alkaline conditions and are water-soluble. So to maximize the intake of these vitamins, food sources should be prepared, cooked and served quickly. For example, steaming vegetables reduces the amount of time they are exposed to heat and minimizes vitamin loss in the cooking water.

VITAMIN D

Needed for the absorption of calcium and the regulation of calcium levels in the blood. Sunlight activates the metabolism of vitamin D in the body.

GOOD SOURCES OF VITAMIN D Butter, margarine, cheese, cream, yogurt, milk, eggs, sunlight.

VITAMIN E

An anti-oxidant that protects the cells from attack by reactive forms of oxygen and free radicals. Involved in red blood cell formation.

GOOD SOURCES OF VITAMIN E Vegetable oils, nuts and nut oils, seeds, egg yolk, margarine, Parmesan, Cheddar, chickpeas, soya beans (and soya products such as TVP, tofu and soya milk), wheat germ, oatmeal, avocados, olives, carrots, parsnips, red peppers, green leafy vegetables, sweet potatoes, tomatoes, sweetcorn, watercress.

VITAMIN K

Needed for effective blood clotting. A deficiency is rare due to bacterial synthesis within the body. Vitamin K is found in most vegetables.

Minerals

Minerals perform a variety of important functions in the human body. A balanced intake is important for long-term good health. Excess of any mineral can be as dangerous as too little.

CALCIUM

Calcium is the most abundant mineral in the body, and is needed for building strong bones and teeth, for muscle contraction and blood clotting. Healthy bones are not only reliant on a good calcium intake but on regular exercise and vitamin D, which aids calcium absorption.

It should also be noted, however, that too much calcium can also be harmful as the excess is deposited in internal organs such as kidneys. This can cause serious problems and even be fatal.

Dairy foods have traditionally been thought of as the principal source of calcium, but have you ever stopped to think where the cow gets its calcium from – certainly not from dairy products!

GOOD SOURCES OF CALCIUM Milk, cheese, yogurt, sesame seeds, tofu, bread, nuts, pulses, okra, broccoli, watercress, onions, green leafy vegetables, sea vegetables, dried fruit such as raisins, apricots, pears and peaches, rhubarb, lemons, oranges, hard water.

MAGNESIUM

Needed for strong bones, and for the functioning of some of the enzymes involved in energy utilization.

GOOD SOURCES OF MAGNESIUM Cream, yogurt, cheese, eggs, bread, papadums, wheat bran, bulgar wheat, oatmeal, soya flour, wholemeal flour, brown rice, wholemeal pasta, nuts, seeds, pulses, green leafy vegetables, sea vegetables, dried fruit such as apricots, pears and peaches.

IRON

Essential component of haemoglobin, the red pigment in blood which transports oxygen though the body. Iron also assists in the production of red blood corpuscles, the metabolism of B vitamins and the functioning of several enzymes. Iron deficiency, which causes anaemia, is the most prevalent nutritional problem worldwide. It has been shown that vegetarians are no more likely to suffer from it than non-vegetarians. A good intake of vitamin C enhances absorption of iron.

GOOD SOURCES OF IRON Eggs, pulses, wholemeal bread, wheat bran, papadums, cashew nuts, pine nuts, pumpkin seeds, cumin seeds, sesame seeds, green leafy vegetables, watercress, sea vegetables, basil, mint, parsley, blackcurrants, dried fruits such as raisins, prunes, figs and peaches, cocoa.

ZINC

Present in every part of the body and vital for the healthy working of many of its functions, including a major role in enzyme reactions, the immune system and resistance to infection. It plays a crucial role in growth and cell division, in insulin activity and liver function. Men need more zinc than women because semen contains 100 times more zinc than is found in the blood, and so the more sexually active a man is, the more zinc he will require.

GOOD SOURCES OF ZINC Cheese, egg yolk, pulses, wholemeal bread, wheat bran, soya flour, yeast, nuts, pumpkin seeds, sesame seeds, tahini paste, green vegetables, garlic.

POTASSIUM

Important in maintaining the body's correct balance of fluids, required for nerve and muscle function, and the metabolism of sugar and protein.

GOOD SOURCES OF POTASSIUM Yogurt, pulses, soya flour, nuts, seeds, green vegetables, potatoes, beetroot, chillies, garlic, sea vegetables, rhubarb, bananas, dates, dried apricots, prunes.

Bibliography

Beyond Beef, *Jeremy Rifkin (Penguin)* • Diet for a New America, *John Robbins (Stillpoint)* • Why You Don't Need Meat, *Peter Cox (Thorsons)* • Fit for Life, *Harvey and Marilyn Diamond (Bantam)* • Diet for a Small Planet, *Frances Moore Lappé (Ballantine)* • Agricultural Statistics 1989, *United States Department of Agriculture, Washington DC* • State of the World's Children, *UNICEF* • The Worldwatch Institute, *cited by Boyce Rensberger, New York Times (25 October 1974)* • Soil and Water, *"Water Requirements for Food Production", Tom Aldridge and Herb Schlubach, Fall 1978, no.38, University of California Cooperative Extension* • Journal of the American Medical Association, *"Premature Mortality from Coronary Heart Disease: The Gramingham Study", T. Gordon* • American Journal of Clinical Nutrition, *"Nutritional Studies of Vegetarians IV: Dietary Acids and Serum Cholesterol Levels", M. Hardinge* • Revista de Biologgia Tropical, *"Forest to Pasture: Development or Destruction?", James Parsons, Vol.24 (supp.1), 1976* • The British Medical Journal, *"Risk of Death from Cancer and Ischaemic Heart Disease in Meat and Non-meat Eaters", Vol.308, pp 1667-74* • Diet, Nutrition and the Prevention of Chronic Diseases, *The World Health Organisation Study Group*

Index

Apple: pie, 170
  sponge pudding, 170
artichoke: dip, 157
  soup, 30
  vegetable paella, 59
asparagus: soup, 25
  with garlic, 44
aubergine: casserole, 66
  caviar, 40
  char-grilled, 121
  mushroom moussaka, 70
  potato and aubergine curry, 102
  spaghettini with tomatoes and, 90
  with sweet peppers, 40
avocado: and mozzarella salad, 134
  guacamole, 157

Bakewell tart, 167
balsamic garlic and herb
  dressing, 146
bananas, praline, 127
barbecue sauce, 153
beans: burgers, 55
  chilli non carne, 55
  green bean salad, 141
  hot pot with butter beans, 61
  lemon green beans, 44
  Mexican rice and, 97
  parsnip and butter bean soup, 20
  pasta and bean salad, 142
  refried bean dip, 156
  quesadillas, 33
  savoury vegetable strudel, 110
  spicy bean jackets, 106
  spicy refried bean tacos, 35
  tacos with red peppers, 35
  technicolor salad, 142
  Tuscan bean and cabbage soup, 19
béchamel sauce, 155
beetroot: borscht, 22
  salad, 140
blue cheese dressing, 147
blueberry tart, 168
borscht, Russian, 22
bread, Mexican corn, 34
broccoli: light vegetable tempura, 43
  purée, 46
  rice noodles with, 99

savoury vegetable strudel, 110
tart with cheese, 115
burgers, 55, 119
burritos, 33
butterscotch, peaches and, 127

Cabbage: potato and cabbage
  mash, 106
  Tuscan bean and cabbage soup, 19
  vegetable soup, 19
Caesar salad, 133
carrot: cake, 172
  garden soup, 26
  layered vegetable terrine, 81
  salad, 134
  soup with potatoes, 17
  summer stew, 76
  vegetable soup, 19
casseroles: aubergine and herb, 66
  cottage crunch, 67
cauliflower: dhal, 74
  layered vegetable terrine, 81
  light vegetable tempura, 43
  salad with mustard
  mayonnaise, 140
  summer stew, 76
  vegetable soufflé, 82
celery: green soup, 22
  vegetable soup, 19
cheese: and broccoli tart, 115
  and nut pâté, 47
  aubergines with sweet peppers, 40
  avocado and mozzarella salad, 134
  blue cheese dressing, 147
  cottage crunch casserole, 67
  enchiladas, 39
  goat's cheese and dill soufflé, 82
  macaroni special, 93
  noodle bake, 60
  palmiers, 48
  pasta salad with pecorino, 142
  penne with mozzarella, 89
  rice and vegetable cheese
  bake, 100
  rocket salad with Parmesan, 129
  sauce with parsley, 155
  savoury vegetable strudel, 110
  spinach and cheese pie, 113

spinach fusilli bake, 92
spinach pancakes with
  mushrooms, 79
straws, 48
stuffed baked potatoes, 101
summer lasagne, 85
traditional enchiladas, 38
warm goat's cheese salad, 133
cheesecake, redcurrant, 166
chick peas: curried with onions, 75
  tomato salad with, 129
chilli: non carne, 55
  salsa, 152
  sauce, 152
  spaghettini with tomatoes and, 90
  spicy dip, 156
  using chillies, 38
chimichangas, 33
chocolate: baked chocolate
  pudding, 162
  chip cookies, 176
  delight, 163
  mousse, 159
  Victoria sponge with butter
  icing, 175
corn bread, Mexican, 34
courgettes: cottage casserole, 67
  light vegetable tempura, 43
  pasta shells with leeks and, 86
  rice and cheese bake, 100
  salad, 141
  savoury vegetable strudel, 110
  soup with watercress, 26
  summer lasagne, 85
  summer stew, 76
  vegetable quiche, 113
  with herbs, 124
  with sweetcorn, 43
crème brûlée, 163
croutons, 30, 136
cucumber: dip, 156
  gazpacho Andaluz, 28
curry: chick peas with onions, 75
  pasta salad, 144
  potato and aubergine, 102
  spicy bean jackets, 106
  spicy raw mushroom salad, 136
  vegetable, 74

Dhal, cauliflower, 74
dill: cucumber dip, 156
  goat's cheese and dill soufflé, 82
  summery tomato soup with, 28
dumplings, 31

Eggs: Chinese egg fried rice, 94
  omelettes, 83
  party, 49
  Provençal pepper salad, 139
enchiladas, 38-9

Fennel salad, 134
fettuccine with creamy tomatoes, 89
filo: cheese straws, 48
  mushroom parcels, 50
  mushroom pie, 109
floating islands, 171
frozen vanilla mousse, 159
fruit: cake, vegan, 172
  juices, 52
  sorbet, 160
fudge sauce, 162
fusilli, spinach bake, 92

Garden soup with pesto, 26
garlic: asparagus with, 44
  balsamic garlic dressing, 146
  beetroot salad with, 140
  char-grilled mushrooms with, 120
  croutons, 136
  mashed potatoes, 106
  mustard dressing, 146
  rice noodles with broccoli and, 99
gazpacho Andaluz, 28
ginger: nuts, 176
  rice noodles with broccoli and, 99
gravy, 155
green herb dip, 157
green herb mayonnaise, 150
green soup with parsley, 22
guacamole, 157

Hollandaise, 150

Juices, 52

Kebabs, vegetable, 119

Lancashire hot pot, 61
lasagne: summer, 85
  winter, 92
leeks: cottage crunch casserole, 67

creamy potato and leek bake, 102
  garden soup, 26
  Greek rice with, 96
  macaroni special, 93
  pasta shells with courgettes
   and, 86
  puffs, 116
  purée with potato, 46
  vegetable soup, 19
lemon: drizzle cake, 175
  green beans, 44
  lemony caper vinaigrette, 147
  soufflé tart, 167
lentils: cauliflower dhal, 74
  soup, 17
lettuce: Caesar salad, 133
  garden soup, 26
  potato and cos lettuce, 130
  warm goat's cheese salad, 133

Macaroni special, 93
mayonnaise, 150
meatballs, meatless, 73
meatless: Bolognese sauce, 154
  loaf, 62
  meatballs with sauces, 73
mille-feuilles, vegetable, 116
mince, vegetarian: casserole, 67
  meatless loaf, 62
  meatless meatballs, 73
  mushroom moussaka, 70
  pasties, 112
  shepherd's pie, 101
  stir-fry with rice, 100
  tacos with tomatoes and, 34
  traditional enchiladas, 38
  winter lasagne, 92
moussaka, mushroom, 70
mousse: chocolate, 159
  frozen vanilla, 159
  raspberry, 160
mushrooms: char-grilled, 120
  cottage crunch casserole, 67
  country, 125
  crisp filo mushroom parcels, 50
  crispy layers, 71
  filo pie, 109
  light vegetable tempura, 43
  meatless loaf, 62
  meatless Stroganoff, 68
  mixed wild mushroom sauce, 154
  moussaka, 70
  risotto, 99
  roasted peppers with, 139

spicy raw mushroom salad, 136
  spinach pancakes with, 79
  tagliatelle with mushroom
   sauce, 88
  triangles, 50
  vegetable paella, 59
  winter lasagne, 92

Nachos, 33
noodles: bake, 60
  vegetable stir-fry with, 56
nuts: cheese and nut pâté, 47
  cottage crunch casserole, 67
  crispy mushroom layers, 71
  grilled nut-topped tomatoes, 121
  pasta twists with spinach and, 88
  praline bananas, 127

Oat and raisin biscuits, 177
omelettes, 83
onions: curried chick peas with, 75
  dealing with, 62
orange rice salad, 144

Paella, vegetable, 59
palmiers, cheese, 48
pancakes, spinach with
  mushrooms, 79
parsnip and butter bean soup, 20
party eggs, 49
pasta: and bean salad, 142
  curried pasta salad, 144
  shells with leeks and
   courgettes, 86
  twists with spinach and nuts, 88
pasties, classic, 112
pastry, 178-9
pâté, cheese and nut, 47
peach: and butterscotch, 127
  cobbler, 168
peas, split: green soup, 22
peas, green: garden soup, 26
pecan pie, 166
penne with tomatoes and
  mozzarella, 89
peppers: aubergines with sweet, 40
  bean tacos with red peppers, 35
  gazpacho Andaluz, 28
  Provençal salad, 139
  rice and vegetable cheese
   bake, 100
  roasted red pepper sauce, 149
  roasted with mushrooms, 139
  stuffed, 68
  vegetable paella, 59

pesto: garden soup with, 26
  sauce, 149
pizza, easy, 117
plum cobbler, 168
poppy seed dressing, 146
potatoes: and cabbage mash, 106
  creamy potato and leek bake, 102
  crispy potato skins, 105
  crusty garlic, 125
  curry with aubergines, 102
  garlic mashed, 106
  hot pot with butter beans, 61
  leek and potato purée, 46
  mushroom moussaka, 70
  rosti, 107
  sage and cream jackets, 124
  salad, 130
  salad with cos lettuce, 130
  savoury fried, 107
  scalloped, 107
  shepherd's pie, 101
  soup with carrots, 17
  spicy bean jackets, 106
  stuffed baked, 101
  summer stew, 76
  sweetcorn chowder, 25
  vegetable soup, 19
praline bananas, 127
pumpkin soup, 20
purées, vegetable, 46
quesadillas, 33

Quiche, vegetable, 113

Raspberry mousse, 160
redcurrant cheesecake, 166
rice: and vegetable cheese bake, 100
  egg fried, 94
  Greek, with leeks, 96
  Mexican with beans, 97
  mushroom risotto, 99
  noodles with broccoli, 93
  orange rice salad, 144
  Persian chilau, 96
  saffron, 94
  Spanish, 97
  stuffed peppers, 68
  types, 99
  vegetable paella, 59
  vegetarian mince stir-fry, 100
risotto, mushroom, 99
rocket: roasted peppers with, 139
  salad, 129
rosti, 107

Saffron rice, 94
sage and cream jackets, 124
salad dressings, 145-7
salsa, 152
sausages: light sausage rolls, 49
  marinated sausages and
    burgers, 119
  toad in the hole, 63
shepherd's pie, 101
sorbet, fruit, 160
soufflé: goat's cheese and dill, 82
  vegetable, 82
soured cream: beetroot salad
    with, 140
  dip, 156
  enchiladas, 39
soy and lemon dressing, 147
spaghetti with olive oil and garlic, 86
spaghettini with sun-dried
    tomatoes, 90
spinach: creamed purée, 46
  fettuccine with creamy
    tomatoes, 89
  fusilli bake, 92
  layered vegetable terrine, 81
  pancakes with mushrooms, 79
  pasta twists with nuts and, 88
  pie with cheese, 113
  rocket salad with Parmesan
    and, 129
  winter lasagne, 92
sponge pudding: apple, 170
  with apricots and almonds, 171
spring rolls, vegetable, 110
steak chunks, vegetarian:
  hot pot with butter beans, 61
  potato and aubergine curry, 102
  quick meatless Stroganoff, 68
stew, summer with vegetables, 76
stir-fry with noodles, 56
stock, vegetable, 31
strudel, savoury vegetable, 110
sweet and sour sauce, 153
sweet potatoes, sauté of, 105
sweetcorn: baked pudding, 60
  chowder, 25
  courgettes with, 43
  Mexican corn bread, 34
  rice and vegetable cheese
    bake, 100

Tacos, 33
  bean, with red peppers, 35
  spicy refried bean, 35

with tomatoes and vegetarian
    mince, 34
tagliatelle with mushroom sauce, 88
tarragon and mustard sauce, 149
tempura, light vegetable, 43
terrine, layered vegetable, 81
thousand island dressing, 147
tiramisù, 162
toad in the hole, 63
tomatoes: aubergine casserole, 66
  fettuccine with creamy, 89
  gazpacho Andaluz, 28
  grilled nut-topped, 121
  light tomato sauce, 151
  penne with mozzarella and, 89
  rich tomato sauce, 151
  salad with avocado, 134
  salsa, 152
  spaghettini with sun-dried, 90
  spinach fusilli bake, 92
  summer lasagne, 85
  summery tomato soup, 28
  sun-dried tomato salad, 129
  tacos with vegetarian mince
    and, 34
  winter lasagne, 92
tortillas, 33

Vanilla mousse, frozen, 159
vegetable: cheese bake and rice, 100
  creamy pie, 112
  curry, 74
  grilled marinated, 120
  juices, 52
  kebabs, 119
  mille-feuilles, 116
  paella, 59
  purées, 46
  quiche, 113
  savoury strudel, 110
  soufflé, 82
  soup, 19
  spring rolls, 110
  stir-fry with noodles, 56
  stock, 31
  tempura, 43
  terrine, 81
vinaigrette, 146

Watercress: and courgette soup, 26
  salad with garlic croutons, 136

Yogurt dressing, 147
Yorkshire puddings, 63